Mathematics
for Key Stage Three

The topic-based tests in this book are a brilliant way to stay on top of the KS3 Maths skills you'll need throughout Years 7-9 (ages 11-14) — and each one will only take up 10 minutes of your life!

This is **Book Two**, which covers everything you'll study in KS3 Maths, except the simplest material (that's in Book One), and the most challenging (which you'll find in Book Three).

10-Minute Tests
Book Two

Contents

Number

Test 1 2
Test 2 4
Test 3 6
Test 4 8
Test 5 10
Test 6 12
Test 7 14
Test 8 16
Test 9 18

Ratio, Proportion and Rates of Change

Test 1 20
Test 2 22
Test 3 24
Test 4 26

Algebra

Test 1 28
Test 2 30
Test 3 32
Test 4 34
Test 5 36
Test 6 38

Geometry and Measures

Test 1 40
Test 2 42
Test 3 44
Test 4 46
Test 5 48
Test 6 50
Test 7 52
Test 8 54

Probability and Statistics

Test 1 56
Test 2 58
Test 3 60
Test 4 62

Answers 64
Progress Charts 71

Published by CGP

Editors: Shaun Harrogate, Ceara Hayden, Caley Simpson

With thanks to Alastair Duncombe and David Ryan for the proofreading.

ISBN: 978 1 78294 481 2

Printed by Elanders Ltd, Newcastle upon Tyne.
Clipart from Corel®
Based on the classic CGP style created by Richard Parsons

Text, design, layout and original illustrations © Coordination Group Publications Ltd. (CGP) 2015
All rights reserved.

Photocopying this book is not permitted, even if you have a CLA licence.
Extra copies are available from CGP with next day delivery • 0800 1712 712 • www.cgpbooks.co.uk

Number: Test 1

Give yourself **10 minutes** to do this test — there are **7 questions** to answer.

Quick-fire Questions

1. What is 0.19 as a fraction?

   A $\frac{19}{10}$

   B $\frac{19}{100}$

   C $\frac{1}{9}$

   (1 mark)

2. What is $\frac{7}{10}$ as a decimal?

   A 0.7

   B 0.07

   C 0.17

   (1 mark)

3. A greengrocer buys nectarines in boxes of 36.

   Without using a calculator, work out how many nectarines there are in 28 boxes.

   ....

   (1 mark)

4. Evaluate the following. Give your answers to 2 decimal places.

   $\sqrt{1679}$

   ....

   (1 mark)

   $\sqrt[3]{583}$

   ....

   (1 mark)

5. **Matthew has 240 songs on his MP3 player. 25% of them are Tina Turner songs.**

   Without using a calculator, work out how many
   Tina Turner songs Matthew has on his MP3 player.

   ....
   (1 mark)

6. **Without using a calculator, work out $\frac{3}{8} \times \frac{11}{9}$.**

   Give your answer as a fraction in its simplest form.

   ....
   (2 marks)

7. **Andy took part in a race. He rowed 1650 m and ran 8.31 km.**

   Without using a calculator, work out how far he travelled in total.
   Give your answer in km.

   .... km
   (2 marks)

   Score: ─── / 10

Number: Test 2

Give yourself **10 minutes** to do this test — there are **7 questions** to answer.

Quick-fire Questions

1. What is 2^3?

   A 6

   B 8

   C 9

   (1 mark)

2. Which number should replace the $\triangle$ in $8^{\triangle} = 64$?

   A 3

   B 8

   C 2

   (1 mark)

3. Which of the numbers in the box below are <u>not</u> prime?

   | 7 | 9 | 19 | 31 | 33 | 45 |

   ....

   (1 mark)

   Find two different prime numbers that add up to 38.

   .... and ....

   (1 mark)

4. Babett buys a new jacket for £17.93. She pays with a £20 note.

   Without using a calculator, work out how much change she gets.

   £ ....

   (1 mark)

Number: Test 2

5. **Work out the following without using a calculator.**

$$\frac{17 + (5 \times 3)}{64 \div (15 - 7)}$$

....
(2 marks)

6. **Juliet is thinking of a number. When she rounds it to 1 decimal place she gets 3.6.**

   What is the smallest possible value of her number?

....
(1 mark)

7. **Tom has 185 plant seeds. A seed tray can hold 12 seeds.**

   Without using a calculator, work out how many seed trays Tom will need in order to plant all of the seeds.

....
(1 mark)

   Tom fills a tray before moving on to the next. How many seeds will there be in the last tray?

....
(1 mark)

Score: ―― / 10

Bonus Brainteaser

Write down all of the prime numbers between 50 and 80.

....

Number: Test 3

Give yourself **10 minutes** to do this test — there are **8 questions** to answer.

Quick-fire Questions

1. What is the answer to 8 − 17?

    A   9

    B   −9

    C   −25

    (1 mark)

2. What is 80 increased by 10%?

    A   88

    B   90

    C   98

    (1 mark)

3. Attila is on holiday abroad. It costs him 15p for every text message he sends.

    Without using a calculator, work out how much it costs him to send 33 text messages on holiday. Give your answer in pounds.

    £ ....
    (1 mark)

4. Look at the numbers below.

    | 4 | 10 | 24 | 26 | 34 | 40 | 48 |

    Write down the numbers from the box that are **not** multiples of 4.

    ....
    (1 mark)

5. Use rounding to estimate the answer to this calculation. Do not use a calculator.

    578 ÷ (38.7 − 11.2)

    ....
    (2 marks)

6. **A minibus can carry a maximum of 7 suitcases.
   32 people each take 3 suitcases on holiday.**

   Without using a calculator, work out how many
   minibuses will be needed to hold everyone's suitcases.

   ....
   (2 marks)

7. **Without using a calculator, find $\sqrt[3]{-27}$.**

   ....
   (1 mark)

8. **There are 450 people on a plane. $\frac{5}{9}$ of them usually get travel sick.**

   Work out how many people on the plane usually get travel sick.

   ....
   (1 mark)

Score: ../10

Number: Test 4

Give yourself **10 minutes** to do this test — there are **7 questions** to answer.

Quick-fire Questions

1. What is 1680 × 100?

    A 16 800

    B 1 680 000

    C 168 000

    (1 mark)

2. 1 954 000 ÷ Δ = 19 540.
   What does Δ equal?

    A 10

    B 100

    C 1000

    (1 mark)

3. Katherine has a set of numbered cards.

    | 7 | 9 | 2 | 8 | 6 |

    What is the closest number to 690 she can make by rearranging the cards?
    She doesn't have to use all of them.

    ....
    (1 mark)

4. The table below shows the number of points Emily, Madeline and John have after a game.

Player	Emily	Madeline	John
Points	8	12	−4

    Without using a calculator, find the difference between
    the number of points that Emily and John have.

    ....
    (1 mark)

5. **Without using a calculator, complete this factor tree for 84.**

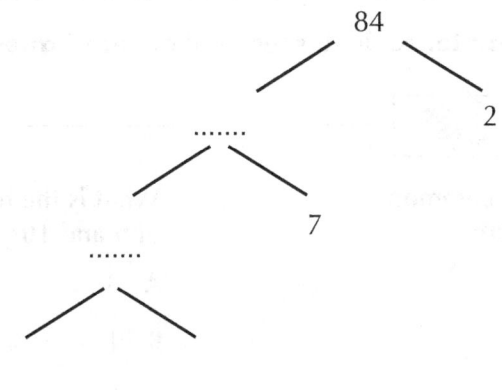

(1 mark)

6. **Work out these calculations without using a calculator.**

   Give your answers in their simplest form, where appropriate.

   $\frac{2}{5} - \frac{1}{3}$

   ....
   (1 mark)

   $\frac{4}{9} + \frac{2}{6}$

   ....
   (2 marks)

7. **Work out the following percentages without using a calculator.**

   28 as a percentage of 400.

   .... %
   (1 mark)

   £300 as a percentage of £250.

   .... %
   (1 mark)

   Score: ──/10

Number: Test 5

Give yourself **10 minutes** to do this test — there are **7 questions** to answer.

Quick-fire Questions

1. What is the lowest common multiple of 8 and 20?

    A 160

    B 4

    C 40

    (1 mark)

2. What is the highest common factor of 9 and 10?

    A 3

    B 1

    C 90

    (1 mark)

3. Lilly travels 13 890 km on her holidays.

   Round this number to the nearest thousand.

   .... km
   (1 mark)

4. Put these numbers in order of size, starting with the smallest.

   | −0.3 | 0.42 | 1.3 | −0.4 | 0.2 |

.... , ... , ... , ... , ...
(1 mark)

5. **Martin's apple tree produced 150 apples last year. 24% of them were rotten.**

   Without using a calculator, work out how many of Martin's apples were rotten.

   .... *(2 marks)*

6. **Without using a calculator, work out the value of the following.**

   $(1 + 3)^3$

   .... *(1 mark)*

   $(2^3)^2$

   .... *(1 mark)*

7. **Rasmus has $\frac{5}{7}$ of a jug of lemonade left. He divides it equally between three glasses.**

   What fraction of the jug of lemonade will be poured into each glass?
   Do not use a calculator.

   .... *(2 marks)*

   Score: ――/10

Bonus Brainteaser

Two thirds of Martin's 150 apples were green. He used one quarter of the green apples to make chutney. How many apples did Martin use to make chutney?

....

Number: Test 6

Give yourself **10 minutes** to do this test — there are **6 questions** to answer.

Quick-fire Questions

1. What is 672 rounded to one significant figure?

   A 700

   B 670

   C 600

   (1 mark)

2. What is 0.00749 rounded to 2 significant figures?

   A 0.01

   B 0.0075

   C 0.007

   (1 mark)

3. A chocolate bar weighs 25.6 g.

   Without using a calculator, work out how much 200 chocolate bars weigh.
   Give your answer in kg.

   .... kg
   (1 mark)

4. Helen goes swimming every eight days. Lee goes swimming every ten days.

   If they both go swimming today, how many days will it be before
   they next go swimming together? Do not use a calculator.

   ....
   (2 marks)

Number: Test 6

5. Write the following numbers in order from smallest to largest.

$\frac{1}{4}$ 0.4   4%   1.4

..................., ..., ..., ...
(2 marks)

6. Write the following as an improper fraction.

$2\frac{3}{5}$

....
(1 mark)

Without using a calculator, use your answer above to calculate $2\frac{3}{5} \div \frac{2}{3}$.
Give your answer as a mixed number in its simplest form.

....
(2 marks)

Score: /10

Number: Test 7

Give yourself **10 minutes** to do this test — there are **8 questions** to answer.

Quick-fire Questions

1. What is $\frac{56}{72}$ in its simplest form?

    A $\frac{8}{9}$

    B $\frac{28}{36}$

    C $\frac{7}{9}$

    (1 mark)

2. What is $3\frac{5}{8}$ as an improper fraction?

    A $\frac{29}{8}$

    B $\frac{35}{8}$

    C $\frac{23}{8}$

    (1 mark)

3. Without using a calculator, work out –6 × 7.

    ....
    (1 mark)

4. Emily walks $\frac{12}{72}$ km to the bus stop.

    Without using a calculator, write this fraction in its simplest form.

    .... km
    (1 mark)

5. Work out $\frac{1}{4} \times \frac{3}{5}$ without using a calculator.

    ....
    (1 mark)

6. **A miniature eclair costs 15p and a vanilla slice costs 34p.
   Georgia buys 60 miniature eclairs. Mitch buys 40 vanilla slices.**

   Without using a calculator, work out how much more Mitch spends than Georgia.
   Give your answer in pounds.

   £ ....
   (2 marks)

7. **Work out $(-1.5)^3$.**

   ....
   (1 mark)

8. **Daniel wants to raise £500 for charity. He has already raised 60% of his target amount.**

   Without using a calculator, work out how much money he has raised already.

   £ ....
   (2 marks)

   Score: —/10

Bonus Brainteaser

Megan also buys some miniature eclairs and 2 vanilla slices from Q6.
She spends a total of £1.58. How many miniature eclairs does she buy?

....

© CGP — not to be photocopied   15   Number: Test 7

Number: Test 8

Give yourself **10 minutes** to do this test — there are **7 questions** to answer.

Quick-fire Questions

1. Which symbol goes in the box below to make the calculation correct?

   36 = 12 ☐ 3

   A ×

   B ÷

   C +

   (1 mark)

2. Which symbol goes in the box below to make the calculation correct?

   18 ☐ (3 × 2) = 12

   A ÷

   B ×

   C −

   (1 mark)

3. Round 6.354 to one decimal place.

   .... *(1 mark)*

4. Phoebe is sorting out her socks.

   $\frac{2}{5}$ of her socks have holes in them.

   What percentage of her sock collection have holes in?

   .... % *(1 mark)*

   20% of her sock collection is blue. What proportion of her sock collection is **not** blue? Give your answer as a decimal.

   .... *(1 mark)*

5. Lucy makes a 400 g lasagne. She eats $\frac{5}{8}$ of it.

   Without using a calculator, work out the number of grams of lasagne she eats.

   .... g
   (1 mark)

6. Without using a calculator, work out the highest common factor of the numbers below.

   6, 18 and 54

   ....
   (2 marks)

7. A café records how many different types of drink it sells over one year.

Drink	Number sold per year
Tea	2.5×10^4
Coffee	1.5×10^5
Hot chocolate	2.6×10^5
Orange juice	3.5×10^4

   Write the number of teas sold as an ordinary number.

   ....
   (1 mark)

   Which drink did the café sell the most of?

   ....
   (1 mark)

   Score: ___ / 10

Number: Test 9

Give yourself **10 minutes** to do this test — there are **7 questions** to answer.

Quick-fire Questions

1. Which sign should go in the box below?

    17.12 ☐ 17.05

    A   <
    B   >
    C   ≤

    (1 mark)

2. How else can the following calculation be written?

    6 × 7 = 42

    A   7 × 42 = 6
    B   42 × 6 = 7
    C   42 ÷ 6 = 7

    (1 mark)

3. Adam rearranges the cards below to make a number.

    | 3 | 6 | 1 | 9 | 7 | 0 |

    What is the largest number he can make?

    ....
    (1 mark)

4. Monika records the amount of water (in litres) she drinks each day during a week at school. Her results are shown below.

    | 1.45 | 1.387 | 1.009 | 1.504 | 1.58 |

    Put the amounts in order, starting with the least amount of water.

    Least water ...., ..., ..., ..., ... Most water

    (1 mark)

5. **Without using a calculator, complete this factor tree for 108.**

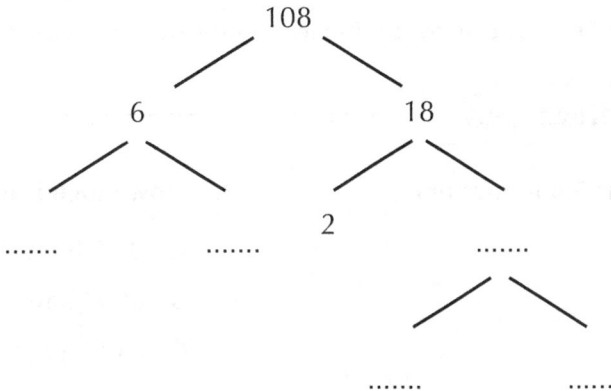

(1 mark)

Now write 108 as a product of its prime factors.

....
(1 mark)

6. Misa paints $\frac{1}{4}$ of a garden gate. Lukas paints $\frac{2}{5}$ of the garden gate.

   What fraction of the garden gate has now been painted?
   Do not use a calculator.

....
(2 marks)

7. **Niki buys 800 ml of orange juice. She drinks 45% of it.**

   Without using a calculator, work out how much orange juice she has left.

   .... ml
   (2 marks)

Score: —/10

Ratio, Proportion and Rates of Change: Test 1

Give yourself **10 minutes** to do this test — there are **7 questions** to answer.

Quick-fire Questions

1. How much is 3.8 tonnes in kg?

   A 3800 kg
   B 380 kg
   C 0.038 kg

   (1 mark)

2. How much is 65 ml in litres?

   A 0.65 litres
   B 6500 litres
   C 0.065 litres

   (1 mark)

3. Koka buys 3 pineapples for £3.60.

   Without using a calculator, work out how much it will cost her to buy 8 pineapples.

   £ ....
   (2 marks)

4. Aimee opens a bank account that pays 2% simple interest each year.

   She decides to put in £320 and leave it untouched for 3 years.
   How much interest will she have earned by the end of the 3 years?

   £ ....
   (2 marks)

5. **Alice roller skates at an average speed of 8 km/h.**

   How far can she skate in 30 minutes?

   .... km
   (1 mark)

6. **Two farmers can shear 20 sheep in 1 hour.**

   Without using a calculator, work out how many sheep 5 farmers would shear in 1 hour at this rate.

   ....
   (1 mark)

7. **At the start of the year, Sarah bought a new mobile phone for £250.
   It decreased in value by 30% over the year.**

   Without using a calculator, work out how much her phone was worth at the end of the year.

   £ ....
   (2 marks)

   Score: —/10

Ratio, Proportion and Rates of Change: Test 2

Give yourself **10 minutes** to do this test — there are **7 questions** to answer.

Quick-fire Questions

1. What is 3 hours 15 minutes in minutes?

   A 195 minutes

   B 315 minutes

   C 205 minutes

   (1 mark)

2. What is 490 seconds in minutes and seconds?

   A 6 minutes 10 seconds

   B 8 minutes 10 seconds

   C 8 minutes 20 seconds

   (1 mark)

3. Rich has three times as many shirts as jumpers.

   Write down the ratio of Rich's shirts to jumpers.
   Give your answer in its simplest form.

   ....
   (1 mark)

4. Rachel can throw a shot put 13 yards.

   Given that 1 yard = 3 feet, what is this distance in feet?

   .... feet
   (1 mark)

   Given that 1 foot ≈ 30 cm, approximately how far can Rachel throw the shot put?
   Give your answer in metres.

   .... m
   (1 mark)

5. A theme park sells two different types of ticket.

    Ride Buster
    £8.50 for 10 rides

    Mega Rider
    £20 for 25 rides

    Which ticket represents the better value for money?

    ....
    (2 marks)

6. Cyril and Shaun share a 630 g curry between them in the ratio 4 : 5.

    Without using a calculator, work out how much curry Shaun gets.

    .... g
    (2 marks)

7. The price of a train ticket from Ulverston to Rugby has increased from £20 to £24.

    Calculate the percentage increase in the ticket price for this journey.

    .... %
    (1 mark)

Score: ▢/10

Bonus Brainteaser

A bus company have just lowered their bus fares by 40%. If a bus ticket from Ulverston to Rugby originally cost £34, how much would it cost now?   £ ....

Ratio, Proportion and Rates of Change: Test 3

Give yourself **10 minutes** to do this test — there are **6 questions** to answer.

Quick-fire Questions

1. Which ratio is the same as 15 : 6?

    A 5 : 3

    B 5 : 2

    C 3 : 2

    (1 mark)

2. Which ratio is the same as 4.2 : 2.1?

    A 2 : 1

    B 42 : 20

    C 4 : 1

    (1 mark)

3. Peter has a map, as shown below. The scale of his map is 1 cm = 1.5 km.

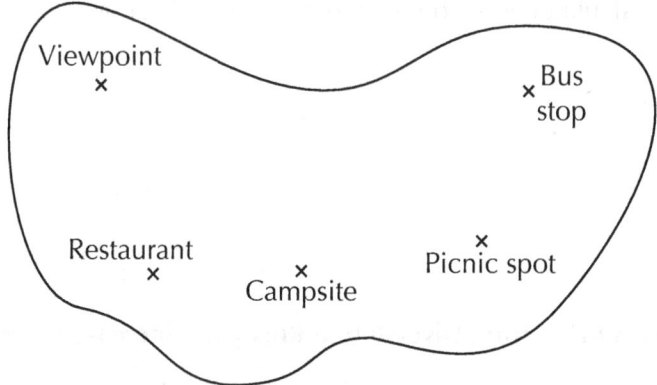

   Work out the real-life distance between the campsite and the bus stop.

   .... km
   (1 mark)

   Peter walks in a direct line from the viewpoint to the picnic spot. He stops after 3 km to tie his shoelace. Mark a cross (×) on the map to show where he stopped.

   (1 mark)

4. Klari uses 3 litres of petrol to travel 60 km. How many litres of petrol will she need in order to travel 240 km?

Do not use a calculator.

.... litres
(2 marks)

5. Convert the following measurements.

4 km into cm

.... cm
(1 mark)

2500 mm² into cm²

.... cm²
(1 mark)

6. A pet store compares how many rabbits and guinea pigs it sells each year. Last year, they sold 40 rabbits. They sold 35% more guinea pigs than rabbits.

How many guinea pigs did the pet store sell last year?

....
(2 marks)

Score: 10

Ratio, Proportion and Rates of Change: Test 4

Give yourself **10 minutes** to do this test — there are **6 questions** to answer.

Quick-fire Questions

1. A map has a scale of 5 cm : 1 m.
    What real-life distance is
    represented by 35 cm on the map?

    A   7 m

    B   7 cm

    C   5 m

    (1 mark)

2. A map has a scale 1 : 10.
    What real-life distance is
    represented by 2.5 cm on the map?

    A   2.5 m

    B   250 m

    C   25 cm

    (1 mark)

3. Duluth and Norcross are 70 km apart. Ralph wants to cycle between the two towns.
    He sets off from Duluth at 9 am and cycles at an average speed of 20 km/h.

    Without using a calculator, work out what time Ralph will arrive in Norcross.

    ....
    (2 marks)

4. It takes Mary 15 minutes to ice 4 cupcakes.

    Without using a calculator, work out how many cupcakes she can ice in 1.5 hours.

    ....
    (2 marks)

5. **The number and types of animal at Broughton Zoo are shown below.**

Animal	Number of animals
Meerkats	8
Alpacas	4
Lemurs	3

Write down the ratio of lemurs to alpacas.

....
(1 mark)

Write down the number of meerkats as a fraction of all the animals at the zoo.

....
(1 mark)

6. **A paddling pool contained 800 litres of water at the start of the summer. At the end of the summer, it contained 600 litres of water.**

Work out the percentage decrease in the amount of water in the paddling pool over the summer.

.... %
(2 marks)

Score: ☐/10

Bonus Brainteaser

Mary has a recipe for 10 cupcakes that uses 150 g of flour.
How much flour will she need to make 32 cupcakes?

.... g

Algebra: Test 1

Give yourself **10 minutes** to do this test — there are **6 questions** to answer.

Quick-fire Questions

1. How many terms are there in the expression $7x + yz - 3$?

   A 2

   B 3

   C 1

   (1 mark)

2. $a + 2b + 5a - b$ simplified is...

   A $6a + b$

   B $4a + b$

   C $6a - b$

   (1 mark)

3. The lines A-E are drawn on the graph below.

   Write down the letter of the graph that matches each equation.

   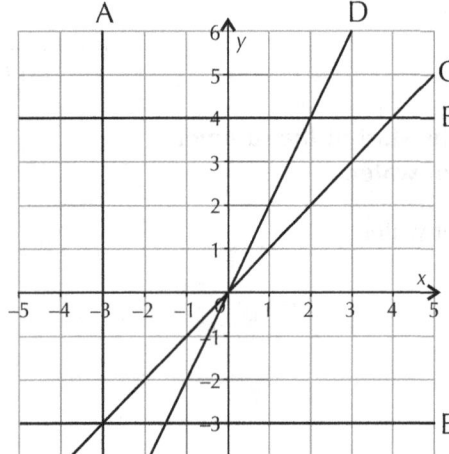

   $x = -3$ ....

   $y = -3$ ....

   $y = 4$ ....

   $y = 2x$ ....

   $y = x$ ....

   (2 marks)

4. Ruth has her own catering business. The formula below is used to work out how much she charges (£C) given the number of people at an event (p).

   $$C = 5p + 10$$

   How much does Ruth charge for an event catering for 20 people?

   £ ....

   (1 mark)

Algebra: Test 1

5. **The graph below shows Lubo's bus journey to the cinema.**

    He catches the bus at 16:00. He gets off the bus at the supermarket to buy sweets and then catches another bus to the cinema to watch a film. After that, Lubo takes a final bus home.

    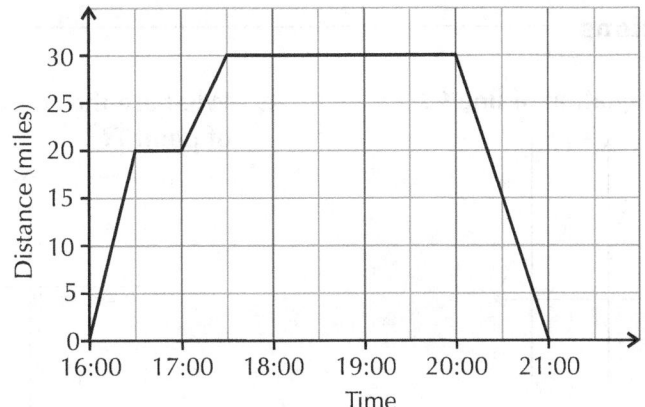

    How far did Lubo travel on the first bus he caught?

    .... miles
    (1 mark)

    How long did Lubo spend at the cinema?

    .... hours and .... minutes
    (1 mark)

6. **Below are the first three patterns of a sequence.**

    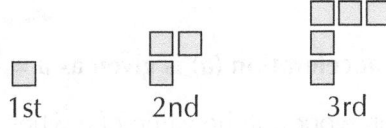

    How many squares will there be in the sixth pattern?

    ....
    (1 mark)

    Find the expression for the number of squares in the *n*th pattern.

    ....
    (2 marks)

    Score: —/10

Algebra: Test 2

Give yourself **10 minutes** to do this test — there are **8 questions** to answer.

Quick-fire Questions

1. What is the equation of line C?

   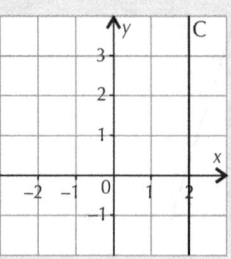

   A $x = -2$ **B** $x = 2$ **C** $y = 2$
   (1 mark)

2. What are the coordinates of point T?

   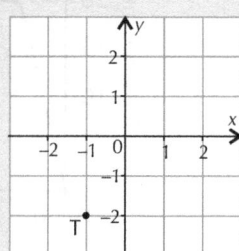

   A $(-2, -1)$ **B** $(-1, -2)$ **C** $(-2, 1)$
   (1 mark)

3. Solve the equation below for *x* without using a calculator.

   $53.5 + x = 92.8$

   $x = $ ....
   (1 mark)

4. The formula to calculate acceleration (a) is given as $a = \dfrac{(v - u)}{t}$.

   Without using a calculator, work out the value of *a* when $v = 26$, $u = 2$ and $t = 12$.

   $a = $ ....
   (1 mark)

5. Rearrange the formula below to make *p* the subject.

   $h = 3p - 2$

   ....
   (1 mark)

6. **The *n*th term of a sequence is given by 3*n* + 2.**

   Without using a calculator, write down the first three terms of the sequence.

   ...., ..., ...
   (1 mark)

7. **Find the gradient of the line below.**

   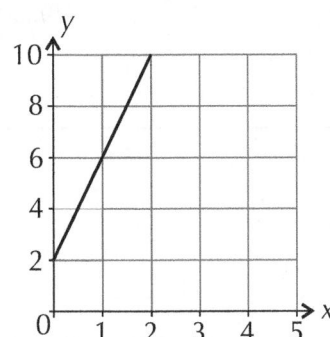

   ....
   (2 marks)

8. **Expand the expression shown below. Simplify your answer.**

   $(s + 2)(s - 3)$

   ....
   (2 marks)

   Score: —/10

   Bonus Brainteaser

   On the grid in Q7, draw a line with gradient –1 which passes through the point (3, 0).

   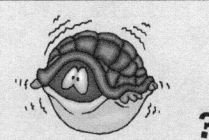

Algebra: Test 3

Give yourself **10 minutes** to do this test — there are **7 questions** to answer.

Quick-fire Questions

1. How else can the equation $y + x = 3$ be written?

   A $x = 3 + y$

   B $x = 3 - y$

   C $y = 3 + x$

   (1 mark)

2. Factorising $6bc + 2b$ gives...

   A $2b(3c + 1)$

   B $b(6c + 2b)$

   C $2(3c + b)$

   (1 mark)

3. Simplify the following expression.

   $3xy + 4x - 2xy - y$

   ....
   (1 mark)

4. The rule for a sequence is "double the previous term and then add 1".

   Use this rule to write down the next three terms of a sequence that starts with 2.

   2, ... , ... , ...
   (2 marks)

5. Solve the following equation for w.

   $4w - 2 = 14$

   $w = $ ....
   (1 mark)

Algebra: Test 3

6. The equation of a straight line is $y = 2x + 2$.

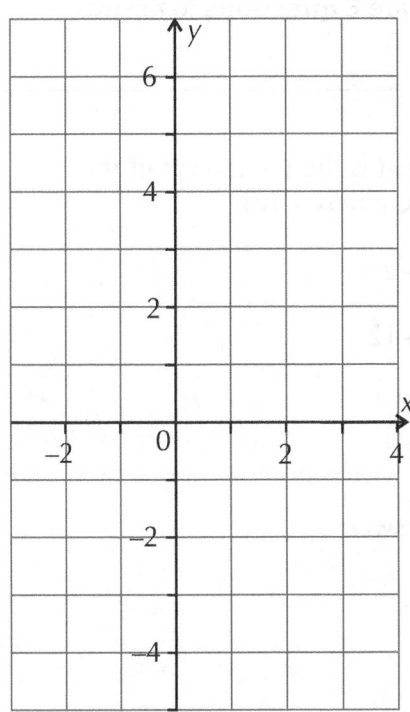

Complete the table of values below for the equation $y = 2x + 2$.

x	−1	0	1	2
y				

(1 mark)

Use your table to draw the graph of $y = 2x + 2$ on the grid to the left.

(1 mark)

7. Three equations of straight line graphs are shown below.

$y = x$ $x + y = 1$ $x − y = 1$

Which line goes through the point (0, 1)?

....

(1 mark)

Which line goes through the origin?

....

(1 mark)

Score: 10

Algebra: Test 4

Give yourself **10 minutes** to do this test — there are **6 questions** to answer.

Quick-fire Questions

1. What is the gradient of the line $y = 2x + 4$?

   A 2

   B 4

   C $\frac{1}{2}$

   (1 mark)

2. What is the *y*-intercept of the line $y = 6x - 12$?

   A -2

   B -12

   C 2

   (1 mark)

3. Expand the expression shown below. Simplify your answer.

   $12(d - 3) + 6d(5d - 2)$

   ....
   (2 marks)

4. The graph below shows how much sponsorship money Claire raises given the distance she manages to run.

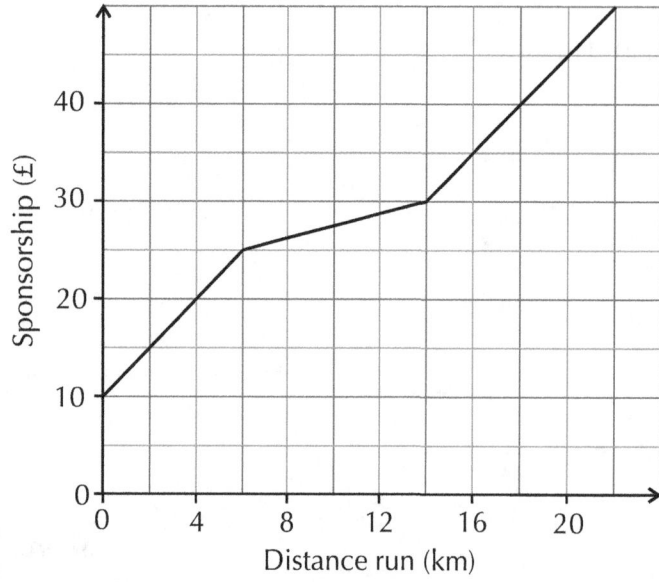

   How far would Claire have run if she raised £25?

   .... km
   (1 mark)

   How much more would Claire raise if she ran 20 km rather than 14 km?

   £ ....
   (1 mark)

5. **Here is a table of values for the equation** $y = x^2 + 2$.

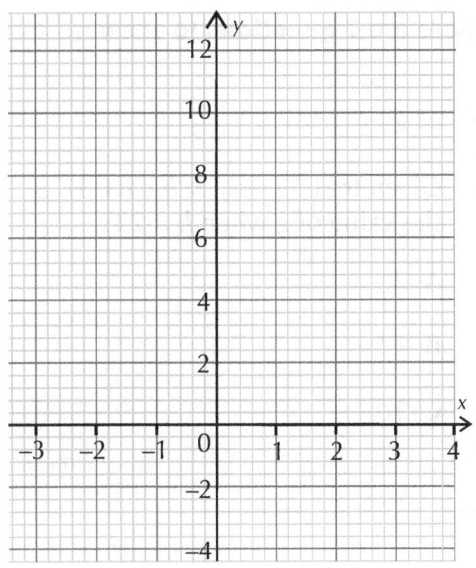

x	−3	−2	−1	0	1	2	3
y	11	6	3				

Complete the table of values above.

(1 mark)

Now use the table to draw the graph of $y = x^2 + 2$.

(1 mark)

6. **Below are the first three patterns of a sequence made from matchsticks.**

  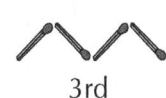
1st   2nd   3rd

Find the expression for the number of matchsticks in the *n*th pattern.

....

(2 marks)

Score: /10

Bonus Brainteaser

Use the graph in Q5 to estimate the values of x when $x^2 + 2 = 4$.
Give your answers to 1 decimal place.

x = ... and ....

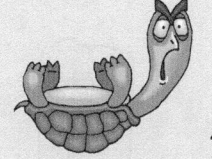

Algebra: Test 5

Give yourself **10 minutes** to do this test — there are **7 questions** to answer.

Quick-fire Questions

1. Multiplying out the brackets in 2(3x + 4) gives...

   A 5x + 8

   B 2x + 8

   C 6x + 8

   (1 mark)

2. Given that 5g + 12 = h what is the value of g when h = 22?

   A 2

   B 12

   C 10

   (1 mark)

3. Use the grid below to answer this question.

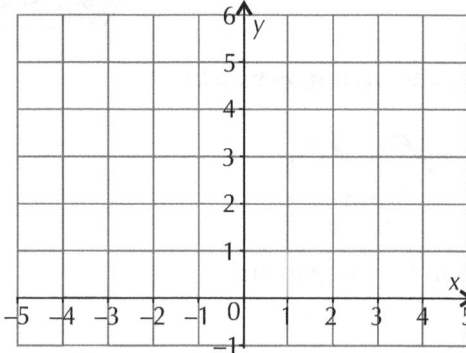

   Plot the following points on the grid:

   A (–4, 0)   **B** (2, 3)   **C** (0, 5)

   (1 mark)

4. A sequence is given below.

   4, 5, 7, 11, 19 ...

   Fill in the missing parts of the rule used to describe the sequence.

   "Multiply the previous term by .... then .... 3."

   (1 mark)

5. **A regular hexagon has sides *x* cm long.**

   Write a formula for the perimeter (*P*) of this regular hexagon.

   ....
   (1 mark)

   Use your formula to calculate the perimeter of a regular hexagon with sides 4 cm long.

   .... cm
   (1 mark)

6. **The graph below shows an exponential graph.**

   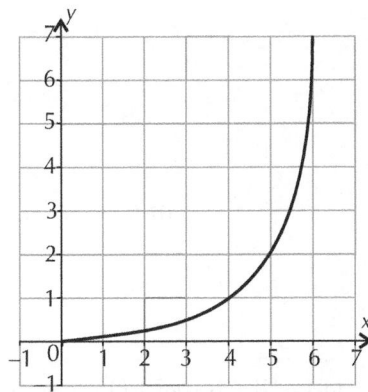

   Use the graph to find the value of *y* when *x* = 4.

   y = ...
   (1 mark)

   Use the graph to find the value of *x* when *y* = 2.

   x = ...
   (1 mark)

7. **The straight line AB passes through the points (–1, 5) and (–3, 6).**

   Without using a calculator, work out the gradient of the line AB.

   ....
   (2 marks)

   Score: ▭/10

Algebra: Test 6

Give yourself **10 minutes** to do this test — there are **6 questions** to answer.

Quick-fire Questions

1. What is the next number in this sequence?

   7, 4, 1, –2, ...

   A –4

   B –5

   C –3

   (1 mark)

2. What is the next number in this sequence?

   1, 2, 4, 8, ...

   A 16

   B 12

   C 10

   (1 mark)

3. Solve the following equation to find *m*.

   $\frac{m+1}{3} = 2$

   m = ...
   (2 marks)

4. Jo has her own cleaning business.
   The amount she earns is shown on the graph below.

   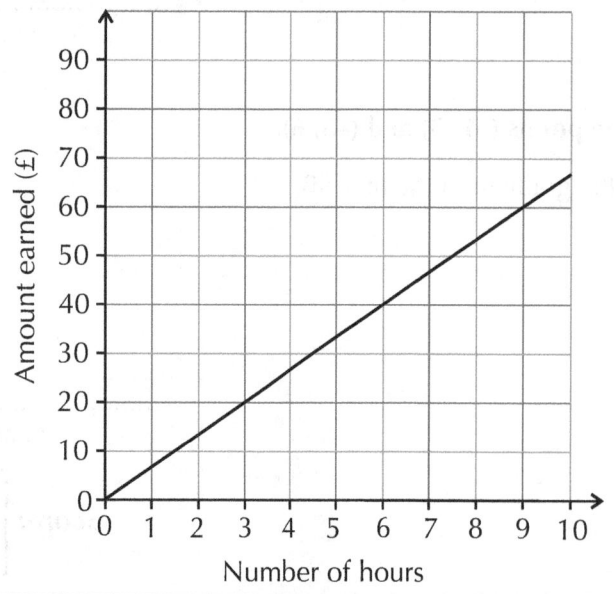

   How much would Jo earn if she cleaned for 3 hours?

   £ ....
   (1 mark)

   Jo earned £60 in one week. How many hours did she clean that week?

   .... hours
   (1 mark)

Algebra: Test 6

5. **Look at the formula below.**

$$F = ma$$

Without using a calculator,
work out the value of F when $m = 2.5$ and $a = 6$.

F = ...
(1 mark)

6. **Look at the line on the grid below.**

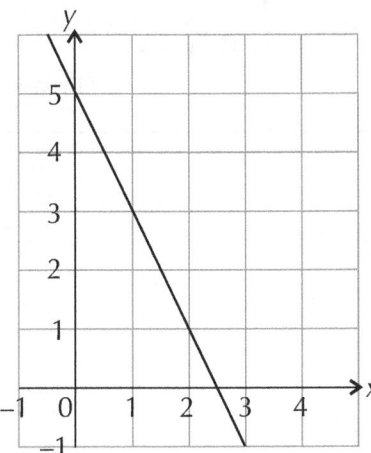

Write down the coordinates of
the y-intercept of the line.

....
(1 mark)

Work out the gradient of the line.

....
(1 mark)

Give the equation of the line in the form $y = mx + c$.

....
(1 mark)

Score: ☐/10

Bonus Brainteaser

Using the formula in Q5, work out
the value of a when $F = 24$ and $m = 3$.

a = ...

Geometry and Measures: Test 1

Give yourself **10 minutes** to do this test — there are **7 questions** to answer.

Quick-fire Questions

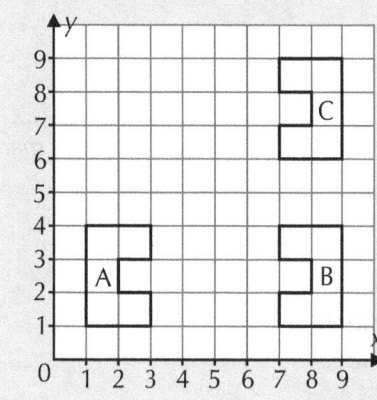

1. What is the equation of the mirror line that reflects shape A onto shape B?

   A $y = 5$ **B** $x = 5$ **C** $y = x$

   (1 mark)

2. What is the equation of the mirror line that reflects shape C onto shape B?

   A $y = 5$ **B** $x = 5$ **C** $y = x$

   (1 mark)

3. Shade in three more squares on the grid below so that it has rotational symmetry of order 2.

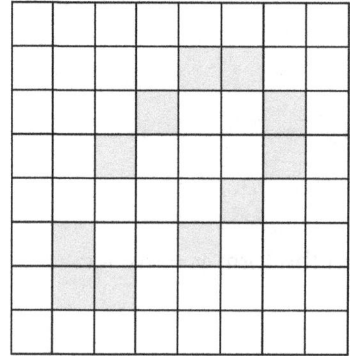

   (1 mark)

4. The area of the hexagonal face of a prism is 28 cm² and the length of the prism is 30 cm.

   What is the volume of the prism?

   .... cm³
   (1 mark)

5. Find the missing angles in the triangle below.

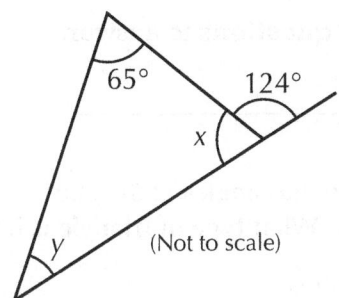

(Not to scale)

x = ...°
(1 mark)

y = ...°
(1 mark)

6. The diagram below shows the net of a cuboid.

   Calculate the perimeter of the net.

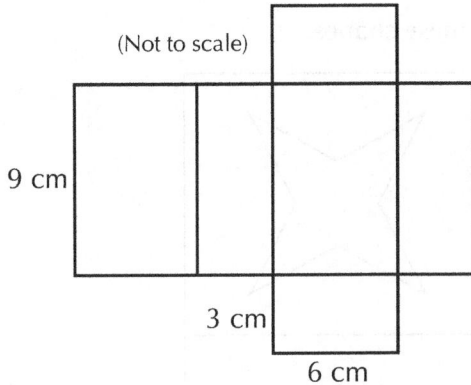

(Not to scale)

.... cm
(2 marks)

7. Find the length of side *a* in the triangle below. Give your answer to 3 significant figures.

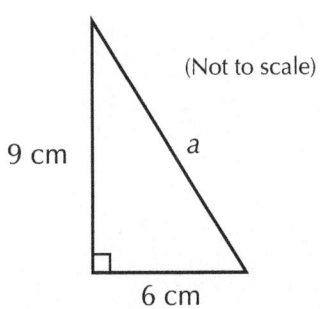

(Not to scale)

a = ... cm
(2 marks)

Score: ☐/10

Geometry and Measures: Test 2

Give yourself **10 minutes** to do this test — there are **7 questions** to answer.

Quick-fire Questions

1. How many vertices does the prism below have?

   A 5
   B 10
   C 15

   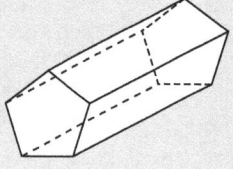

   (1 mark)

2. A triangle has angles of 50°, 80° and 50°. What type of triangle is it?

   A isosceles
   B right-angled
   C scalene

   (1 mark)

3. Find the order of rotational symmetry of each of these shapes.

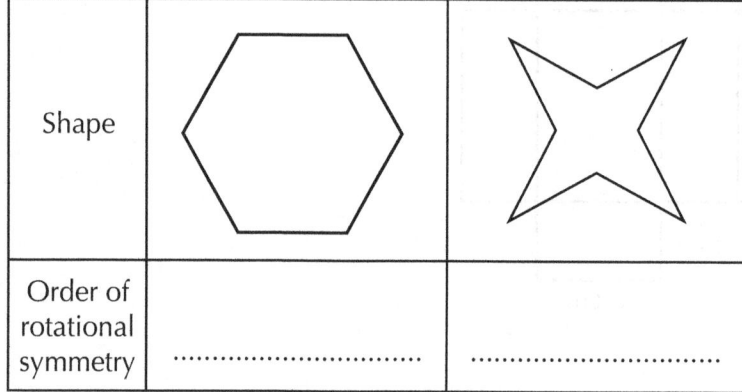

(1 mark)

4. Construct the bisector of angle ABC below.

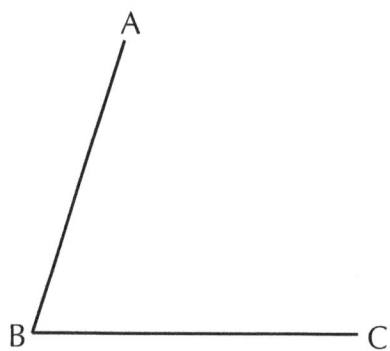

(2 marks)

5. **A decagon is a 10-sided shape.**

   Calculate the sum of the interior angles in a decagon.

   .... °
   (1 mark)

6. **The shape below is made by joining a semicircle and a triangle.**
   The radius of the semicircle is 2 cm and the height of the triangle is 7 cm.

   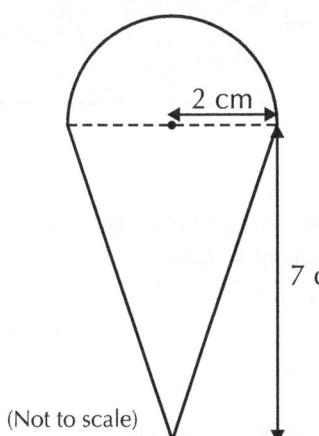

   Calculate the total area of the shape.
   Give your answer to 2 decimal places.

   .... cm²
   (2 marks)

7. **Shape ABCDE is made up from an isosceles triangle ABE and a parallelogram BCDE.**

   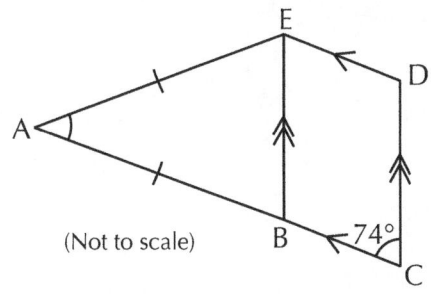

   ABC is a straight line and angle BCD = 74°.
   Without using a calculator,
   work out the size of angle BAE.

   .... °
   (2 marks)

   Score: ―― / 10

Geometry and Measures: Test 3

Give yourself **10 minutes** to do this test — there are **6 questions** to answer.

Quick-fire Questions

1. What is the name of this shape?

   A   trapezium
   B   kite
   C   rhombus

   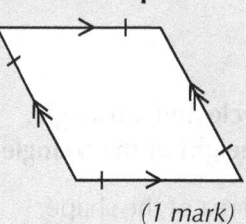

   (1 mark)

2. What 3D shape is formed by this net?

   A   tetrahedron
   B   triangular prism
   C   cone

   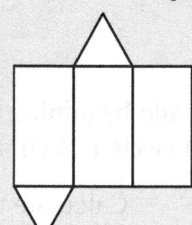

   (1 mark)

3. Shape D and point A are shown on the grid below.

   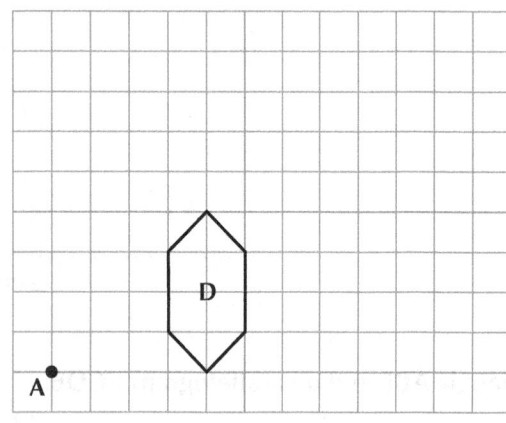

   Enlarge shape D by a scale factor of 2 using point A as the centre of enlargement. Label the image C.

   (1 mark)

   Draw all the lines of symmetry on shape C.

   (1 mark)

4. Find the size of angle *h* in the triangle below.

   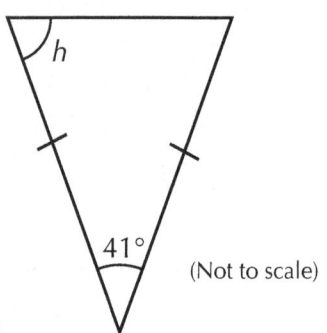

   (Not to scale)

   $h = $ ....°

   (2 marks)

Geometry and Measures: Test 3   44   © CGP — not to be photocopied

5. Joan's patio is in the shape of a circle as shown below. It has a radius of 4.5 m.

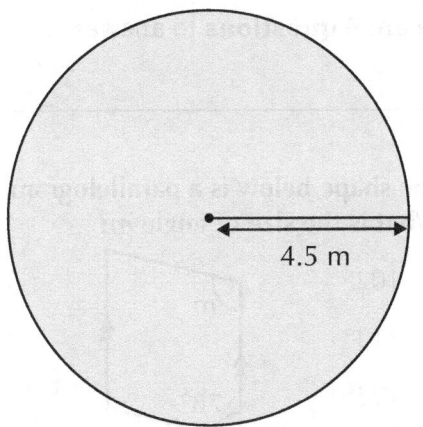

Find the circumference of Joan's patio.
Give your answer to 2 decimal places.

.... m
(2 marks)

6. Cleo is constructing an equilateral triangle ABC with side lengths of 6 cm. So far she has only drawn line AB.

Use a pair of compasses to complete Cleo's construction.

A •————————————• B

(2 marks)

Score: ☐/10

Bonus Brainteaser

Joan from Q5 wants to replace her patio with turf.
Turf comes in 5 m² rolls. How many rolls will she need?

.... rolls

Geometry and Measures: Test 4

Give yourself **10 minutes** to do this test — there are **6 questions** to answer.

Quick-fire Questions

1. What is the size of the missing angle in the shape below?

   A 60°
   B 70°
   C 80°

   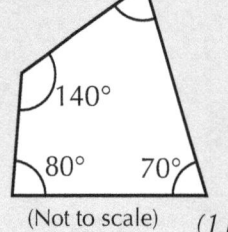
   (Not to scale) *(1 mark)*

2. The shape below is a parallelogram. What is the size of angle *m*?

   A 102°
   B 112°
   C 122°

   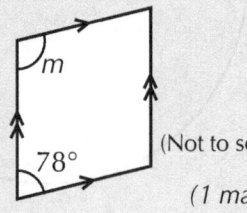
   (Not to scale)
   (1 mark)

3. Which shapes in the box below are similar to shape A?

   ....
   (1 mark)

4. On the grid below, shape Q is an enlargement of shape P.

   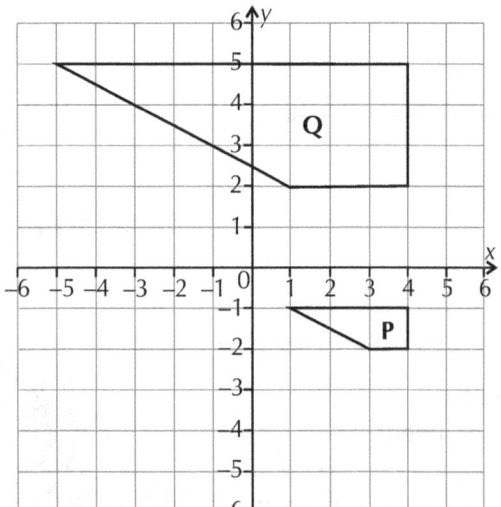

   What is the scale factor of the enlargement?

   ....
   (1 mark)

   What is the centre of enlargement?

   ....
   (1 mark)

Geometry and Measures: Test 4

5. **The cuboid on the right has side lengths of 5 cm, 8 cm and 10 cm.**

   Calculate the surface area of the cuboid.

   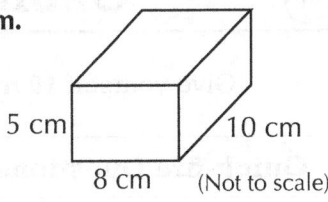

   .... cm²

   (2 marks)

6. **Shapes X and Y are drawn on the grid below.**

   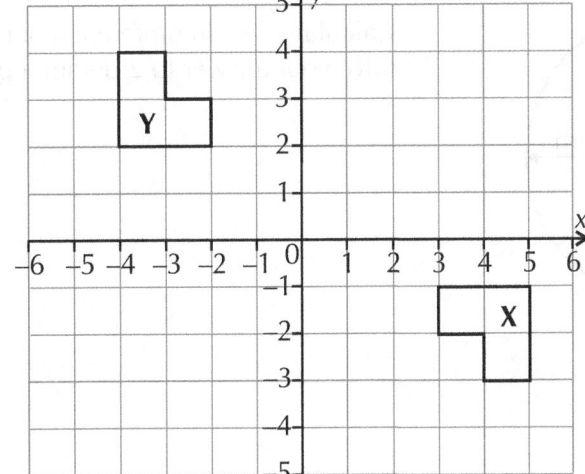

   Rotate shape X 90° clockwise about the point (0, 1). Label the image Z.

   (1 mark)

   Describe the rotation that maps shape Y onto shape Z.

   ....

   ....

   (2 marks)

   Score: ―――
   10

Geometry and Measures: Test 5

Give yourself **10 minutes** to do this test — there are **6 questions** to answer.

Quick-fire Questions

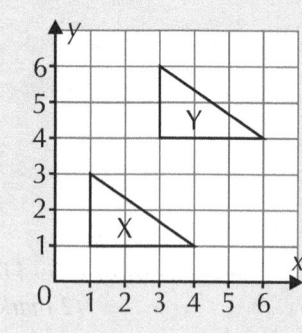

1. Which of these vectors translates shape X onto shape Y?

   A $\begin{pmatrix} 2 \\ 3 \end{pmatrix}$ B $\begin{pmatrix} -2 \\ 3 \end{pmatrix}$ C $\begin{pmatrix} 3 \\ 2 \end{pmatrix}$

   (1 mark)

2. Which of these vectors translates shape Y onto shape X?

   A $\begin{pmatrix} -3 \\ -2 \end{pmatrix}$ B $\begin{pmatrix} 2 \\ -3 \end{pmatrix}$ C $\begin{pmatrix} -2 \\ -3 \end{pmatrix}$

   (1 mark)

3. A children's playground has a circular roundabout with a radius of 1.8 m.

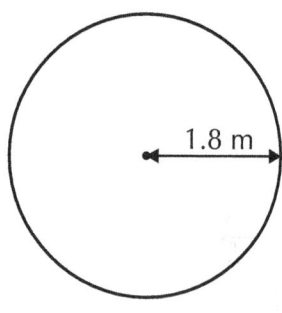

   Calculate the circumference of the roundabout.
   Give your answer to 2 decimal places.

   .... m
   (1 mark)

4. Find the value of *g* in the right-angled triangle below.

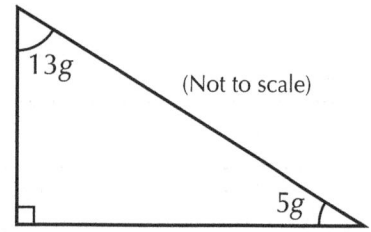

(Not to scale)

   g = ... °
   (2 marks)

5. **The net of a square-based pyramid is shown below.**

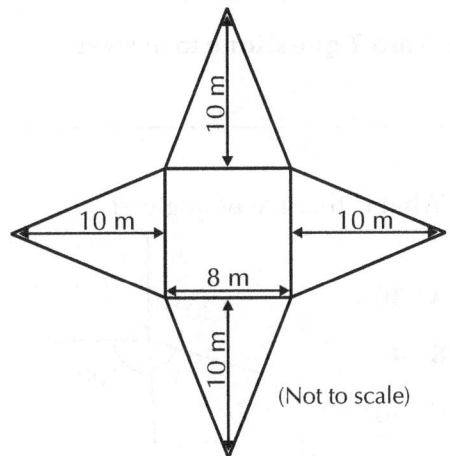

Calculate the surface area of the pyramid.

.... m²
(2 marks)

6. **The diagram below shows two parallelograms between two parallel lines.**

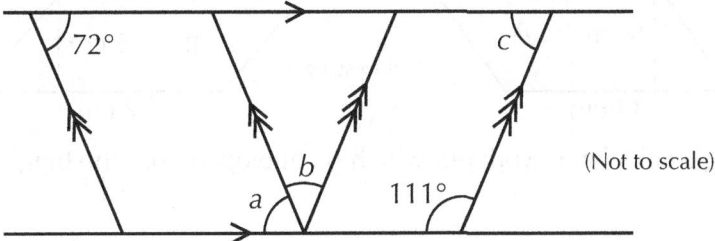

Find the size of the angles *a*, *b* and *c*.

a = ... °

b = ... °

c = ... °
(3 marks)

Score: ──
       10

Bonus Brainteaser

In Q5, the missing side lengths of the triangular faces can be found using Pythagoras' Theorem. Calculate the perimeter of the net.
Give your answer to 3 significant figures.

.... m

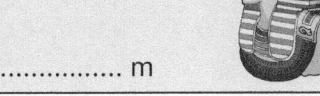

Geometry and Measures: Test 6

Give yourself **10 minutes** to do this test — there are **7 questions** to answer.

Quick-fire Questions

1. What is the size of angle *x*?

   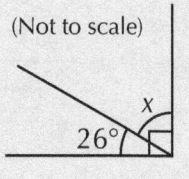

   A 54°   **B** 64°   **C** 74°

2. What is the size of angle *y*?

   A 30°
   B 40°
   C 50°

   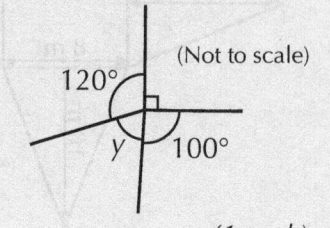

   (1 mark)   *(1 mark)*

3. Parallelograms A and B are shown below.

   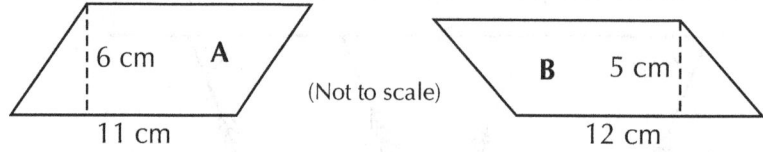

   (Not to scale)

   Without using a calculator, work out which parallelogram has the biggest area.

   ....
   (1 mark)

4. Reflect shape M in the line *y* = 4. Label the reflected shape N.

   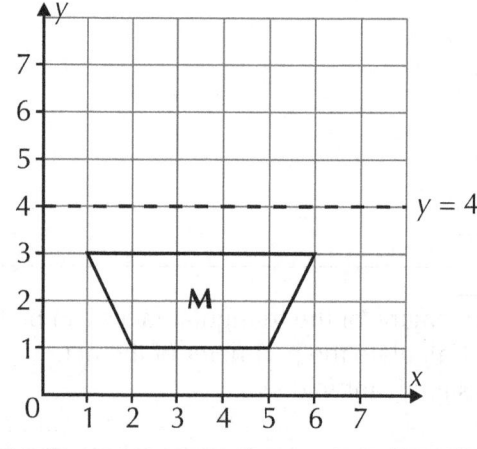

   (1 mark)

5. Find the size of angle GBC in the diagram below. Explain your answer.

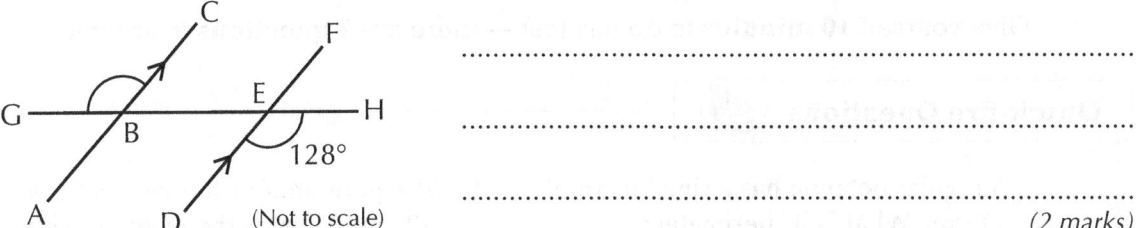

(Not to scale)

....

....

....
(2 marks)

6. Construct the perpendicular bisector of the line WZ below.

(2 marks)

7. A fishing rod, standing on horizontal ground, is leaning against a vertical wall.
The base of the fishing rod is 1.5 m from the wall and it reaches 4 m up the wall.

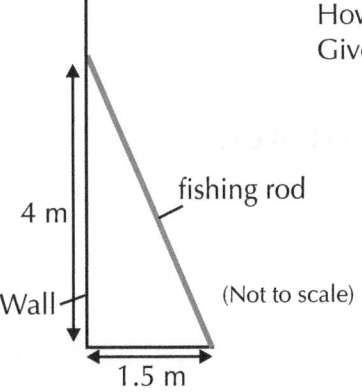

How long is the fishing rod?
Give your answer to 2 decimal places.

(Not to scale)

.... m
(2 marks)

Score: —/10

Geometry and Measures: Test 7

Give yourself **10 minutes** to do this test — there are **7 questions** to answer.

Quick-fire Questions

1. A regular octagon has a side length of 11 cm. What is its perimeter?

   A 80 cm

   B 88 cm

   C 110 cm

   (1 mark)

2. The perimeter of this rectangle is 38 cm. What is the length of side x?

   A 8 cm

   B 9 cm

   C 10 cm

   (1 mark)

3. Shape Q is a reflection of shape P. Draw the mirror line below.

   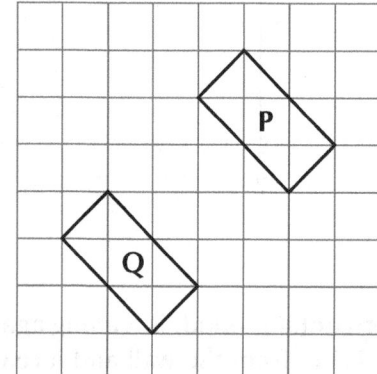

   (1 mark)

4. A cuboid-shaped fish tank has side lengths 80 cm, 40 cm and 30 cm.

   Find the volume of water that the fish tank can hold.

   .... cm³
   (1 mark)

5. Find the area of the triangle below.

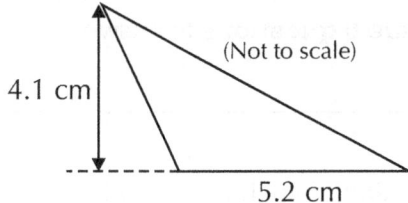

.... cm²
(2 marks)

6. On the grid below, rotate shape T 90° clockwise about the origin.

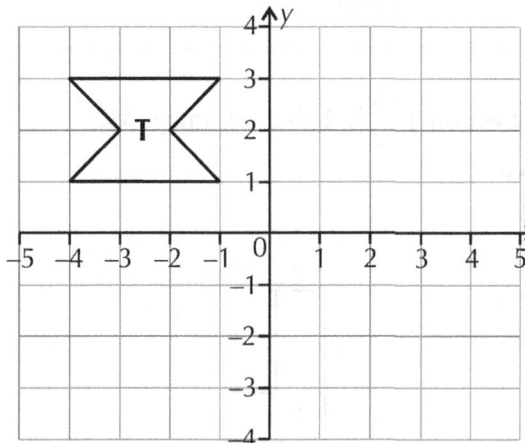

(2 marks)

7. The metal washer shown below is made by drilling a hole through a circular piece of metal with radius 3 cm. The hole has an area of 12 cm².

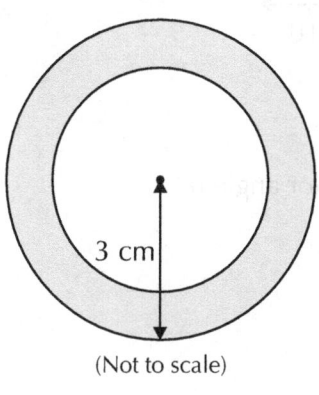

What is the area of the metal washer?
Give your answer to 3 significant figures.

.... cm²
(2 marks)

Score: /10

Geometry and Measures: Test 8

Give yourself **10 minutes** to do this test — there are **6 questions** to answer.

Quick-fire Questions

1. What is the size of angle *z*?

    A 80°
    B 100°
    C 120°

    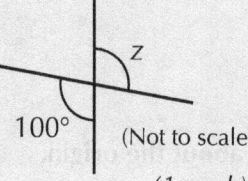
    (Not to scale)

    (1 mark)

2. What kind of angles are *x* and *y*?

    A alternate
    B corresponding
    C vertically opposite

    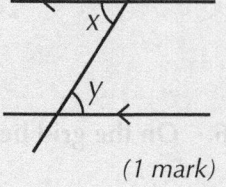

    (1 mark)

3. Translate shape V by the vector $\begin{pmatrix} -3 \\ -2 \end{pmatrix}$. Label the image W.

    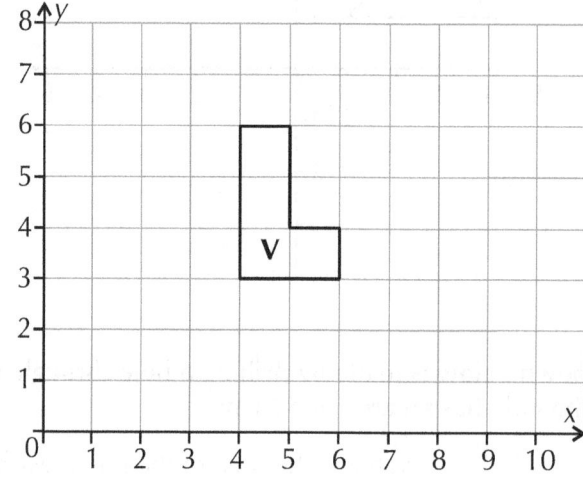

    (1 mark)

4. A regular octagon is shown below.

    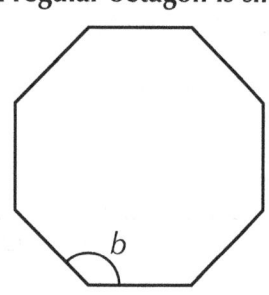

    Calculate the size of the interior angle *b*.

    b = ...°

    (2 marks)

5. **The floor plan of Alastair's living room is shown below.
   It is made up from two trapeziums joined together.**

   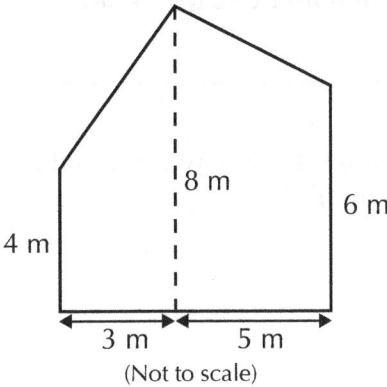
   (Not to scale)

   Calculate the area of his living room floor.

   .... m²
   (2 marks)

6. **A lumberjack chops down a tree and cuts all of the branches off. He's left with
   a tree trunk in the shape of a cylinder with a radius of 50 cm and a length of 7 m.**

   What is the volume of the tree trunk in m³?
   Give your answer to 2 decimal places.

   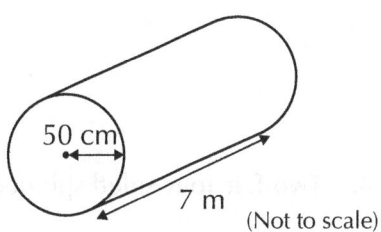
   (Not to scale)

   .... m³
   (3 marks)

   Score: ___ / 10

Bonus Brainteaser

Alastair wants to put a new carpet in his living room from Q5.
The carpet he wants costs £15 per m².
How much will it cost him to carpet his living room?

£ ....

Probability and Statistics: Test 1

Give yourself **10 minutes** to do this test — there are **6 questions** to answer.

Quick-fire Questions

1. P = {factors of 6}.
    Which option shows set P?

    A P = {1, 2, 3, 4, 5, 6}

    B P = {1, 2, 3, 6}

    C P = {1, 6}

    (1 mark)

2. Q = {multiples of 4 between 1 and 25}.
    What is n(Q)?

    A 6

    B 7

    C 8

    (1 mark)

3. Describe the correlation shown by the scatter graph on the right.

   ....
   (1 mark)

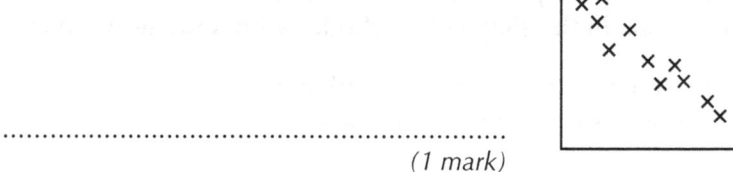

4. Two fair four-sided spinners numbered 1-4 are spun and their scores added together.

   Complete the sample space diagram below to show all the possible outcomes.

	1	2	3	4
1	2	3		
2			5	
3	4			7
4	5	6		8

   (1 mark)

   What is the probability of getting a total of exactly 6?

   ....
   (1 mark)

5. **Kit records the number of pages in 9 different books:**

   80, 87, 96, 75, 65, 88, 76, 82, 91

   What is the range of the number of pages in these books?

   ....
   (1 mark)

   What is the median number of pages in these books?

   ....
   (1 mark)

6. **The students in a dance school were asked what their favourite type of dance was. The results are shown in the pie chart on the right.**

   40 students said they liked tap best.
   How many students are there in the dance school?

   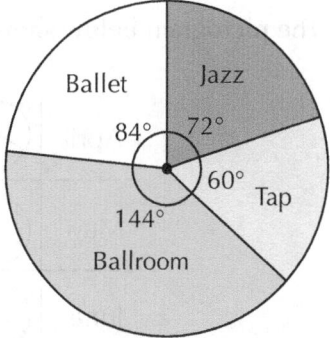

   ....
   (1 mark)

   Use this information to complete the table below.

Favourite type of dance	Jazz	Tap	Ballroom	Ballet
Frequency		40		

   (2 marks)

Probability and Statistics: Test 2

Give yourself **10 minutes** to do this test — there are **6 questions** to answer.

Quick-fire Questions

1. Which word best describes the likelihood that a fair coin lands heads up when tossed once?

   A Impossible

   B Likely

   C Evens

   (1 mark)

2. A fair 8-sided spinner numbered 1-8 is spun once. What is the probability that it lands on a 2 or a 3?

   A 0.2

   B 0.25

   C 0.125

   (1 mark)

3. The pictogram below shows the number of rounds of golf Liz played over 4 months.

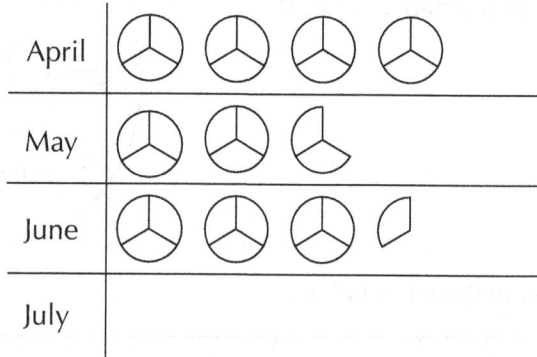

   How many rounds of golf did she play in May?

   ....
   (1 mark)

   In July, she played 7 rounds of golf.
   Complete the pictogram to show this information.

   (1 mark)

4. **This frequency table shows the number of hats owned by the pupils in Class 8B.**

Number of hats	0	1	2	3	4	5
Frequency	5	5	8	7	4	1

What is the modal number of hats owned by the pupils in Class 8B?

....
(1 mark)

How many hats do the pupils in Class 8B own in total?

....
(1 mark)

5. **Shola spins the fair spinner below.**

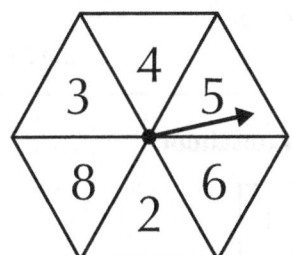

What is the probability that he spins a 5?

....
(1 mark)

What is the probability that he spins an even number?
Give your answer as a fraction in its simplest form.

....
(1 mark)

6. **Eight teachers were asked how long they had been teaching for.**
   The answers, in years, of seven of the teachers were 1, 7, 2, 8, 12, 4 and 3.

The median length for all eight teachers was 5 years.
How many years had the eighth teacher been teaching for?

.... years
(2 marks)

Score: —/10

Bonus Brainteaser

Use the frequency table from Q4 to calculate the mean number of hats owned by Class 8B.

....

Probability and Statistics: Test 3

Give yourself **10 minutes** to do this test — there are **6 questions** to answer.

Quick-fire Questions

A five-sided spinner numbered 1-5 is spun 50 times and the results recorded.

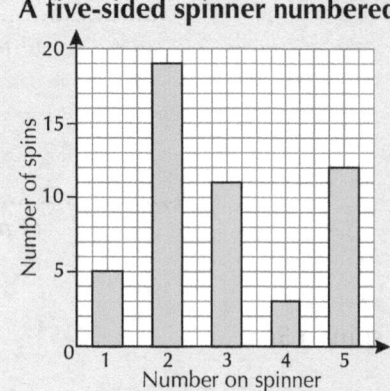

1. What is the relative frequency of the spinner landing on a 2?

   A 0.19   B 0.38   C 0.2

   (1 mark)

2. How many times would you expect the spinner to land on a 2 if it was spun 200 times?

   A 76   B 38   C 40

   (1 mark)

3. Cassie records the time (in minutes) it takes her friends to travel to school:

   8, 15, 21, 16, 9, 5, 75, 23, 12, 14

   Identify the outlier in the data.

   .... minutes
   (1 mark)

4. This frequency table shows the number of times Class 9A went to the cinema in a month.

Number of cinema trips	0	1	2	3	4	5
Frequency	7	10	8	3	1	2

   What is the median number of cinema trips?

   ....
   (2 marks)

5. A shop records the midday temperature (in °C) and the number of BBQs it sells each day for a week. The results are shown in the table below.

Midday temperature (°C)	Number of BBQs sold
10	9
14	13
16	17
18	18
20	20
22	24
23	22

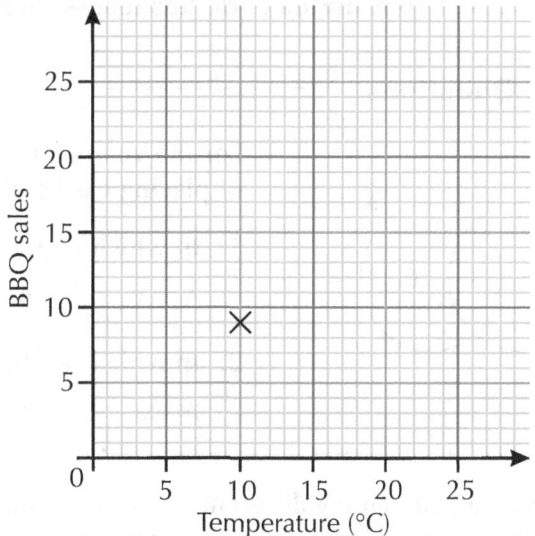

Use the table to complete the scatter graph. The first point has been plotted already.

(1 mark)

Draw a line of best fit on your graph.

(1 mark)

Use your line of best fit to predict the number of BBQs sold in a week when the midday temperature was 12 °C.

....
(1 mark)

6. The pupils in Year 7 were asked what their favourite school trip had been. The results are shown in the pie chart below.

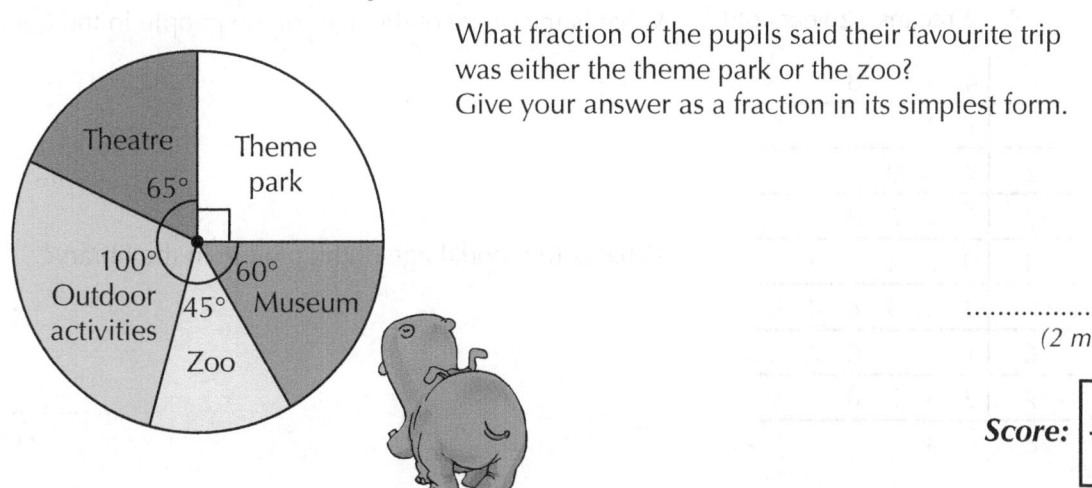

What fraction of the pupils said their favourite trip was either the theme park or the zoo?
Give your answer as a fraction in its simplest form.

....
(2 marks)

Score: ☐/10

Probability and Statistics: Test 4

Give yourself **10 minutes** to do this test — there are **6 questions** to answer.

Quick-fire Questions

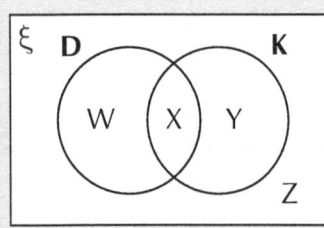

For the Venn diagram on the left, ξ = {a standard pack of playing cards}, D = {diamonds} and K = {kings}

1. In which region should the queen of diamonds go?

   A W   B X   C Y   *(1 mark)*

2. In which region should the ace of clubs go?

   A X   B Y   C Z   *(1 mark)*

3. Aziza has a bag containing different coloured counters. There are 20 counters in total, and 7 of them are red. She picks a counter from the bag at random.

   What is the probability that the counter she picks is <u>not</u> red?

   ....
   (1 mark)

4. Jason records the ages of the people in a library at 11 am on a Saturday morning. The results are shown in the stem and leaf diagram below.

   1 | 2 means 12 years old

0	4 4 7 8
1	1 2 4
2	2 6 9
3	1 4 6 8
4	0 2 4 7 9
5	2 2 3 8 8 8
6	1 3 4 6 7 9
7	2 5 7 8
8	0 4

   What is the range of the ages of the people in the library?

   ....
   (1 mark)

   What is the modal age of the people in the library?

   ....
   (1 mark)

5. A forest ranger has been measuring the average height (ft) of some trees in a forest for five years. He records the results in the table below.

Use the information in the table to draw a line graph to show the average height of the trees in the forest over this time.

Year	Average height of trees (ft)
2010	3
2011	5
2012	12
2013	16
2014	19

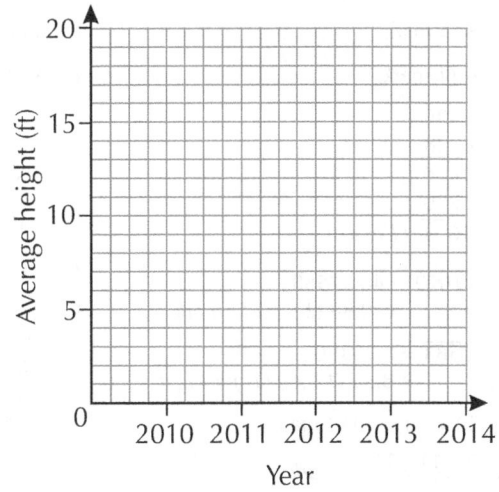

(2 marks)

6. The frequency table below shows the number of holidays 40 people go on in a year.

Number of holidays	0	1	2	3	4	Total
Frequency	6	14	10	6	4	40
Number of holidays × frequency						

Complete the table and use it to find the mean number of holidays per person.

....
(3 marks)

Score: ⎯⎯ / 10

Answers

Number: Test 1

1. B *(1 mark)*
2. A *(1 mark)*
3.
```
    36
  × 28
  ----
   288
   720
  ----
  1008
```
   (1 mark)
4. $\sqrt{1679} = 40.97560...$
   $= 40.98$ (2 d.p.) *(1 mark)*

   $\sqrt[3]{583} = 8.35390...$
   $= 8.35$ (2 d.p.) *(1 mark)*
5. $240 \div 4 = 60$ *(1 mark)*
6. $\frac{3}{8} \times \frac{11}{9} = \frac{33}{72}$ *(1 mark)*
   $= \frac{11}{24}$ *(1 mark)*
7. 1650 m = 1.65 km *(1 mark)*
   1.65 + 8.31 = 9.96 km *(1 mark)*

Number: Test 2

1. B *(1 mark)*
2. C *(1 mark)*
3. 9, 33 and 45 *(1 mark)*
   7 and 31 *(1 mark)*
4.
```
   £20.00
 − £17.93
 --------
 £  2.07
```
   (1 mark)
5. $\frac{17 + (5 \times 3)}{64 \div (15 - 7)} = \frac{17 + 15}{64 \div 8}$ *(1 mark)*
   $= \frac{32}{8} = 4$ *(1 mark)*
6. 3.55 *(1 mark)*
7.
```
      1 5 remainder 5
  12 ⟌1 8 5
```
   Tom will need 16 trays. *(1 mark)*
   There will be 5 seeds in the last tray. *(1 mark)*

BONUS BRAINTEASER
53, 59, 61, 67, 71, 73, 79

Number: Test 3

1. B *(1 mark)*
2. A *(1 mark)*
3.
```
     33
   × 15
   ----
    165
    330
   ----
    495  = £4.95
```
   (1 mark)
4. 10, 26, 34 *(1 mark)*
5. E.g. $578 \div (38.7 - 11.2)$
   $\approx 600 \div (40 - 10)$
   $= 600 \div 30 = 20$
   (2 marks available — 1 mark for suitable rounding, 1 mark for correct answer.)
6. $32 \times 3 = 96$ *(1 mark)*
```
       1 3 remainder 5 minibuses
    7 ⟌9 6
```
   so 14 minibuses will be needed. *(1 mark)*
7. −3 *(1 mark)*
8. $450 \div 9 = 50$
   $50 \times 5 = 250$ *(1 mark)*

Number: Test 4

1. C *(1 mark)*
2. B *(1 mark)*
3. 689 *(1 mark)*
4. $8 - (-4) = 8 + 4 = 12$ *(1 mark)*
5.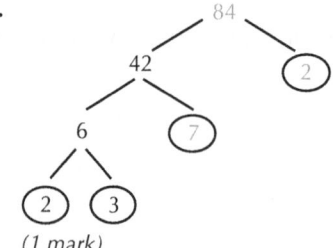
   (1 mark)

6. $\frac{2}{5} - \frac{1}{3} = \frac{6}{15} - \frac{5}{15} = \frac{1}{15}$ *(1 mark)*

   $\frac{4}{9} + \frac{2}{6} = \frac{8}{18} + \frac{6}{18}$ *(1 mark)*
   $= \frac{14}{18} = \frac{7}{9}$ *(1 mark)*

7. $\frac{28}{400} = \frac{7}{100} = 7\%$ *(1 mark)*
   $\frac{300}{250} = 1\frac{50}{250} = 1\frac{20}{100} = 120\%$
   (1 mark)

Number: Test 5

1. C *(1 mark)*
2. B *(1 mark)*
3. 14 000 km *(1 mark)*
4. −0.4, −0.3, 0.2, 0.42, 1.3 *(1 mark)*
5. 10% of 150 = 15
   So 1% of 150 = 1.5
   20% = 30 and 4% = 6
   So 24% of 150 = 30 + 6 = 36
   (2 marks available — 1 mark for a correct method, 1 mark for the correct answer.)
6. $(1 + 3)^3 = 4^3 = 64$ *(1 mark)*
   $(2^3)^2 = 8^2 = 64$ *(1 mark)*
7. $\frac{5}{7} \div 3 = \frac{5}{7} \times \frac{1}{3} = \frac{5}{21}$
   (2 marks available — 1 mark for a correct method, 1 mark for the correct answer.)

BONUS BRAINTEASER
$\frac{2}{3}$ of 150 = 150 ÷ 3 × 2 = 100
100 ÷ 4 = 25

Number: Test 6

1. A *(1 mark)*
2. B *(1 mark)*
3. 200 × 25.6 = 5120 g
   5120 ÷ 1000 = 5.12 kg *(1 mark)*
4. Multiples of 8: 8, 16, 24, 32, ㊵ ...
   Multiples of 10: 10, 20, 30, ㊵ ...
   So they will both go to swimming together after 40 days.
   (2 marks available — 1 mark for using a correct method, 1 mark for the correct answer.)

Answers

5. $\frac{1}{4} = 0.25$, 0.4, 4% = 0.04, 1.4
    Order: 0.04, 0.25, 0.4, 1.4
    = 4%, $\frac{1}{4}$, 0.4, 1.4
    (2 marks available — 1 mark for changing all the numbers into the same form, 1 mark for ordering them correctly.)

6. $2\frac{3}{5} = \frac{13}{5}$ *(1 mark)*
    $\frac{13}{5} \div \frac{2}{3} = \frac{13}{5} \times \frac{3}{2} = \frac{39}{10} = 3\frac{9}{10}$
    (2 marks available — 1 mark for a correct method, 1 mark for the correct answer.)

Number: Test 7

1. C *(1 mark)*
2. A *(1 mark)*
3. −42 *(1 mark)*
4. $\frac{12}{72} = \frac{1}{6}$ km *(1 mark)*
5. $\frac{1}{4} \times \frac{3}{5} = \frac{3}{20}$ *(1 mark)*
6. 15 × 60 = 900p = £9.00
    34 × 40 = 1360p = £13.60
    £13.60 − £9.00 = £4.60
    (2 marks available — 1 mark for both amounts spent, 1 mark for the correct difference.)
7. −3.375 *(1 mark)*
8. 10% of £500 = £50 *(1 mark)*
    so 60% of £500 = £50 × 6 = £300
    (1 mark)

BONUS BRAINTEASER
34p × 2 = 68p
£1.58 − £0.68 = £0.90
£0.90 ÷ £0.15 = 6 miniature eclairs

Number: Test 8

1. A *(1 mark)*
2. C *(1 mark)*
3. 6.4 *(1 mark)*
4. $\frac{2}{5} = 0.4 = 40\%$ *(1 mark)*
    100% − 20% = 80% = 0.8 *(1 mark)*

5. 400 ÷ 8 = 50 g
    50 × 5 = 250 g *(1 mark)*
6. Factors of 6: 1, 2, 3, ⑥
    Factors of 18: 1, 2, 3, ⑥, 9, 18
    Factors of 54: 1, 2, 3, ⑥, 9, 18, 27, 54
    So the HCF of 6, 18 and 54 is 6.
    (2 marks available — 1 mark for using a correct method, 1 mark for the correct answer.)
7. 25 000 *(1 mark)*
    Hot chocolate *(1 mark)*

Number: Test 9

1. B *(1 mark)*
2. C *(1 mark)*
3. 976 310 *(1 mark)*
4. 1.009, 1.387, 1.45, 1.504, 1.58 *(1 mark)*
5.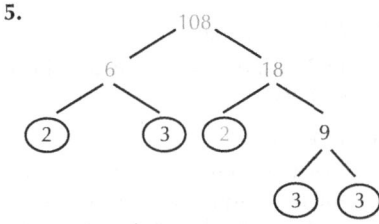
    (1 mark)
    $2 \times 2 \times 3 \times 3 \times 3$ (or $2^2 \times 3^3$)
    (1 mark)
6. $\frac{1}{4} + \frac{2}{5} = \frac{5}{20} + \frac{8}{20} = \frac{13}{20}$
    (2 marks available — 1 mark for a correct method, 1 mark for the correct answer.)
7. 10% of 800 = 80
    So 40% of 800 = 80 × 4 = 320 ml
    5% of 800 = 80 ÷ 2 = 40 ml
    45% = 320 + 40 = 360 ml *(1 mark)*
    So she has 800 − 360 = 440 ml left *(1 mark)*

Ratio, Proportion and Rates of Change: Test 1

1. A *(1 mark)*
2. C *(1 mark)*
3. £3.60 ÷ 3 = £1.20 *(1 mark)*
    8 × £1.20 = £9.60 *(1 mark)*
4. 2% interest = £320 × 0.02
    = £6.40 *(1 mark)*
    £6.40 × 3 = £19.20 *(1 mark)*
5. 30 minutes = 0.5 hours
    8 × 0.5 = 4 km *(1 mark)*
6. 20 ÷ 2 = 10 sheep per farmer per hour
    10 × 5 = 50 sheep *(1 mark)*
7. 10% of £250 = £25
    30% of £250 = £25 × 3 = £75
    (1 mark)
    £250 − £75 = £175 *(1 mark)*

Ratio, Proportion and Rates of Change: Test 2

1. A *(1 mark)*
2. B *(1 mark)*
3. 3 : 1 *(1 mark)*
4. 13 × 3 = 39 feet *(1 mark)*
    39 × 30 = 1170 cm
    = 11.7 m *(1 mark)*
5. Ride Buster: £8.50 ÷ 10
    = £0.85 per ride.
    Mega Rider: £20 ÷ 25
    = £0.80 per ride.
    So the Mega Rider ticket is the better value for money.
    (2 marks available — 1 mark for a correct method, 1 mark for the correct answer.)
6. Total number of parts: 4 + 5 = 9
    One part: 630 ÷ 9 = 70 g *(1 mark)*
    Shaun gets 5 × 70 = 350 g *(1 mark)*
7. £24 − £20 = £4
    (4 ÷ 20) × 100 = 20% *(1 mark)*

BONUS BRAINTEASER
10% of £34 = £3.40
So 40% of £34 = £13.60
£34 − £13.60 = £20.40

Answers

Ratio, Proportion and Rates of Change: Test 3

1. B *(1 mark)*

2. A *(1 mark)*

3. Length on drawing = 4 cm
   4 × 1.5 = 6 km *(1 mark)*
   3 km = 2 cm on map

   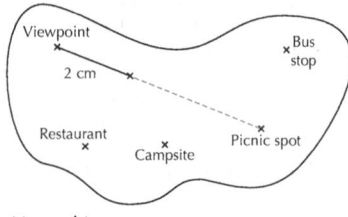

   (1 mark)

4. 240 ÷ 60 = 4 *(1 mark)*
   3 × 4 = 12 litres *(1 mark)*

5. 4 km = 4 × 1000 m
          = 4000 m
   4000 m = 4000 × 100 cm
             = 400 000 cm *(1 mark)*
   2500 mm^2 = 2500 ÷ 10 ÷ 10
             = 25 cm^2 *(1 mark)*

6. 35% = 0.35
   40 × 0.35 = 14
   So 40 + 14 = 54 guinea pigs
   (2 marks available — 1 mark for a correct method, 1 mark for the correct answer.)

Ratio, Proportion and Rates of Change: Test 4

1. A *(1 mark)*

2. C *(1 mark)*

3. 70 ÷ 20 = 3.5 hours *(1 mark)*
   9 am + 3.5 hours = 12:30 pm
   (1 mark)

4. There are 6 lots of 15 minutes in 1.5 hours.
   So 4 × 6 = 24 cupcakes.
   (2 marks available — 1 mark for a correct method, 1 mark for the correct answer.)

5. 3 : 4 *(1 mark)*
   $\frac{8}{15}$ *(1 mark)*

6. 800 − 600 = 200
   (200 ÷ 800) × 100 = 0.25 × 100
                  = 25%
   (2 marks available — 1 mark for a correct method, 1 mark for the correct answer.)

BONUS BRAINTEASER
150 ÷ 10 = 15 g per cupcake
15 × 32 = 480 g

Algebra: Test 1

1. B *(1 mark)*

2. A *(1 mark)*

3. x = −3: A, y = −3: E, y = 4: B,
   y = 2x: D, y = x: C
   (2 marks available — 2 marks for all correct answers, otherwise 1 mark for three correct answers.)

4. C = 5 × 20 + 10
      = 100 + 10 = £110 *(1 mark)*

5. 20 miles *(1 mark)*
   17:30 to 20:00 = 2 hours 30 minutes *(1 mark)*

6. 11 *(1 mark)*
   To get from one pattern to the next, you add 2 squares — so the nth term contains 2n. The 1st pattern has 1 square in, so to get from 2 × 1 = 2 to 1, you subtract 1. So the nth term is 2n − 1.
   (2 marks available — 2 marks for correct answer, otherwise 1 mark for 2n.)

Algebra: Test 2

1. B *(1 mark)*

2. B *(1 mark)*

3. 53.5 + x = 92.8
   x = 92.8 − 53.5
   x = 39.3 *(1 mark)*

4. $a = \frac{(26-2)}{12} = \frac{24}{12} = 2$ *(1 mark)*

5. $p = \frac{h+2}{3}$ *(1 mark)*

6. 5, 8, 11 *(1 mark)*

7. Choose two points, e.g. (1,6) & (0,2)
   Gradient: $\frac{6-2}{1-0} = \frac{4}{1} = 4$
   (2 marks available — 1 mark for a correct method, 1 mark for the correct answer.)

8. (s + 2)(s − 3)
   = $s^2 − 3s + 2s − 6$ *(1 mark)*
   = $s^2 − s − 6$ *(1 mark)*

BONUS BRAINTEASER

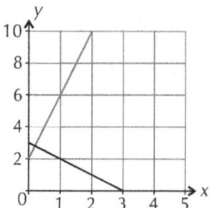

Algebra: Test 3

1. B *(1 mark)*

2. A *(1 mark)*

3. xy + 4x − y *(1 mark)*

4. 2, 5, 11, 23 *(2 marks available — 2 marks for all three correct answers, otherwise 1 mark for any two correct answers.)*

5. 4w = 14 + 2
   4w = 16
   w = 4 *(1 mark)*

6. 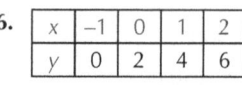 *(1 mark)*

   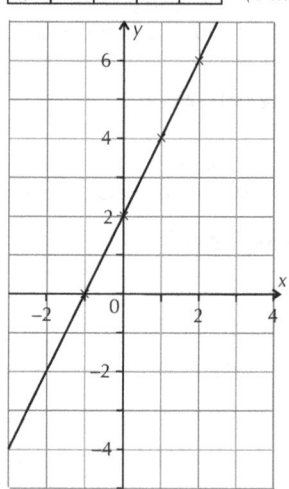

   (1 mark)

Answers

7. Put $x = 0$ into each equation:
    $y = x$: $y = 0$ ✗
    $x + y = 1$: $0 + y = 1$
    so $y = 1$ ✓
    $x - y = 1$: $0 - y = 1$
    so $y = -1$ ✗
    $x + y = 1$ *(1 mark)*
    Put $x = 0$ into each equation:
    $y = x$: $y = 0$ ✓
    $x + y = 1$: $0 + y = 1$
    so $y = 1$ ✗
    $x - y = 1$: $0 - y = 1$
    so $y = -1$ ✗
    $y = x$ *(1 mark)*

Algebra: Test 4:

1. A *(1 mark)*
2. B *(1 mark)*
3. $12d - 36 + 30d^2 - 12d$ *(1 mark)*
   $= 30d^2 - 36$ *(1 mark)*
4. 6 km *(1 mark)*
   £45 − £30 = £15 *(1 mark)*
5.

x	−3	−2	−1	0	1	2	3
y	11	6	3	2	3	6	11

(1 mark)

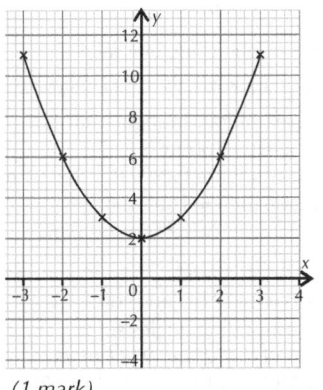

(1 mark)

6. To get from one pattern to the next, you add 1 matchstick — so the *n*th term contains *n*. The 1st pattern has 2 matchsticks in, so to get from 1 × 1 = 1 to 2, you add 1. So the *n*th term is $n + 1$.
    (2 marks available — 2 marks for correct answer, otherwise 1 mark for n.)

BONUS BRAINTEASER
$x = -1.4$ (allow −1.5 or −1.3) and 1.4 (allow 1.3 and 1.5)

Algebra: Test 5

1. C *(1 mark)*
2. A *(1 mark)*
3.

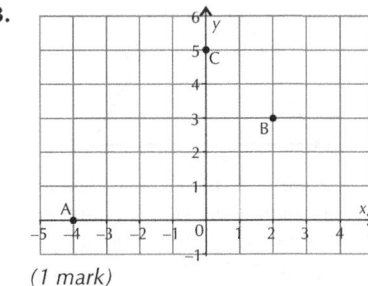

(1 mark)

4. Multiply the previous term by 2 then subtract 3. *(1 mark)*
5. $P = 6x$ *(1 mark)*
   $P = 6 \times 4 = 24$ cm *(1 mark)*
6. $y = 1$ *(1 mark)*
   $x = 5$ *(1 mark)*
7. Gradient of AB: $\frac{6-5}{-3-(-1)}$ *(1 mark)*
   $\frac{1}{-2} = -\frac{1}{2}$ *(1 mark)*

Algebra: Test 6

1. B *(1 mark)*
2. A *(1 mark)*
3. $m + 1 = 6$ *(1 mark)*
   $m = 5$ *(1 mark)*
4. £20 *(1 mark)*
   9 hours *(1 mark)*
5. $F = 2.5 \times 6 = 15$ *(1 mark)*

6. (0, 5) *(1 mark)*
    Two points, e.g. (1,3) and (2, 1)
    So gradient $= \frac{1-3}{2-1} = \frac{-2}{1} = -2$ *(1 mark)*
    $y = -2x + 5$ *(1 mark)*

BONUS BRAINTEASER
$24 = 3a$
$a = 8$

Geometry and Measures: Test 1

1. B *(1 mark)*
2. A *(1 mark)*
3.

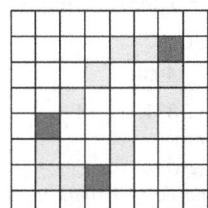

(1 mark)

4. $28 \times 30 = 840$ cm^3 *(1 mark)*
5. $x = 180° - 124° = 56°$ *(1 mark)*
   $y = 180° - 65° - 56° = 59°$ *(1 mark)*
6. $9 + 6 + 3 + 3 + 6 + 3 + 3 + 9 + 3 + 3 + 6 + 3 + 3 + 6 = 66$ cm
   (2 marks available — 1 mark for finding the missing sides of the net, 1 mark for the correct answer.)
7. Use Pythagoras' Theorem:
   $a^2 = 9^2 + 6^2 = 117$ *(1 mark)*
   $a = \sqrt{117} = 10.8166...$ cm
   $= 10.8$ cm (3 s.f.) *(1 mark)*

Geometry and Measures: Test 2

1. B *(1 mark)*
2. A *(1 mark)*
3. 6 and 4 *(1 mark)*

Answers

4.

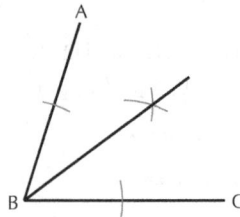

(2 marks available — 1 mark for correctly drawn construction arcs, 1 mark for a correct and accurate angle bisector.)

5. 180 × (10 − 2) = 1440° *(1 mark)*

6. Area of semicircle
= $\frac{1}{2} \times \pi \times 2^2$ = 6.2831... cm²
Area of triangle
= $\frac{1}{2} \times 4 \times 7$ = 14 cm²
Total area = 6.2831... + 14
= 20.2831... cm²
= 20.28 cm² (2 d.p.)
(2 marks available — 1 mark for the area of the semicircle, 1 mark for the area of the triangle and the correct answer.)

7. E.g. Angle ABE = 74° because of corresponding angles.
Angle AEB = 74° because AEB is an isosceles triangle.
Angle BAE = 180° − 74° − 74° = 32°
(2 marks available — 1 mark for finding either angle ABE or angle AEB, 1 mark for the correct answer.)

Geometry and Measures: Test 3

1. C *(1 mark)*

2. B *(1 mark)*

3.
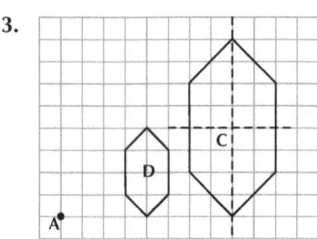

(1 mark for correct enlargement.)
(1 mark for two lines of symmetry.)

4. 180° − 41° = 139° *(1 mark)*
h = 139° ÷ 2 = 69.5° *(1 mark)*

5. Circumference = 2 × 4.5 × π *(1 mark)*
= 28.27433... m
= 28.27 m (2 d.p.) *(1 mark)*

6.
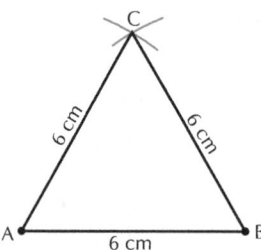

(2 marks available — 1 mark for correctly drawn construction arcs, 1 mark for a correct and accurate equilateral triangle.)

BONUS BRAINTEASER

Area = π × 4.5² = 63.6172... m²
63.6172... ÷ 5 = 12.7234...
So Joan will need 13 rolls of turf.

Geometry and Measures: Test 4

1. B *(1 mark)*

2. A *(1 mark)*

3. C and E *(1 mark)*

4. 3 *(1 mark)*

(4, −4) *(1 mark)*

5. 2(5 × 8) + 2(5 × 10) + 2(8 × 10)
= 340 cm²
(2 marks available — 1 mark for a correct method, 1 mark for the correct answer.)

6.
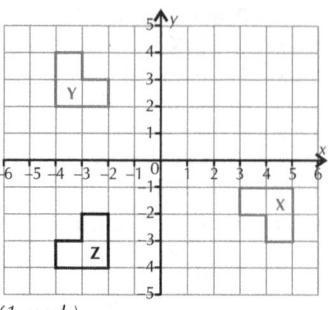

(1 mark)

Rotate shape Y 90° anticlockwise about the origin.
(2 marks available — 1 mark for '90° anticlockwise', 1 mark for 'about the origin' or 'about the point (0, 0)'.)

Geometry and Measures Test 5

1. A *(1 mark)*

2. C *(1 mark)*

3. Circumference = 2 × 1.8 × π
= 11.3097... = 11.31 m (2 d.p.)
(1 mark)

4. 90° + 5g + 13g = 180° *(1 mark)*
18g = 90°
g = 5° *(1 mark)*

5. Area of one triangular face
= $\frac{1}{2} \times 10 \times 8$ = 40 m² *(1 mark)*
So area of four triangular faces
= 4 × 40 = 160 m²
Area of square face = 8 × 8 = 64 m²
Surface area = 160 + 64
= 224 m² *(1 mark)*

6. a = 72° *(1 mark)*
a + b = 111° because of corresponding angles so
b = 111° − 72° = 39° *(1 mark)*
c = 180° − 111° = 69° *(1 mark)*

Answers

BONUS BRAINTEASER
Use Pythagoras' Theorem to find the length of one side of the triangle:
$10^2 + 4^2 = 100 + 16 = 116$
$\sqrt{116} = 10.7703...$ m
Perimeter = $8 \times 10.7703...$
= $86.1626...$ m = 86.2 m (3 s.f.)

Geometry and Measures: Test 6

1. B *(1 mark)*
2. C *(1 mark)*
3. Area A = $11 \times 6 = 66$ cm^2
   Area B = $12 \times 5 = 60$ cm^2
   So A has a bigger area *(1 mark)*
4.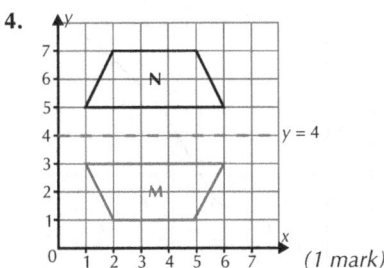
   (1 mark)
5. E.g. Angle ABE = 128° as it is a corresponding angle with DEH *(1 mark)*. Angle GBC = 128° as it is a vertically opposite angle to ABE *(1 mark)*.
6.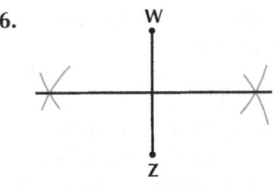
   (2 marks available — 1 mark for correctly drawn construction arcs, 1 mark for a correct and accurate perpendicular bisector.)
7. Use Pythagoras' Theorem:
   $4^2 + 1.5^2 = 18.25$ *(1 mark)*
   $\sqrt{18.25} = 4.2720...$
   = 4.27 m (2 d.p.) *(1 mark)*

Geometry and Measures: Test 7

1. B *(1 mark)*
2. C *(1 mark)*
3.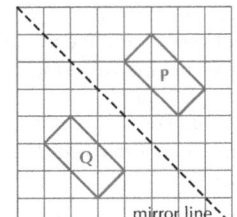
   (1 mark)
4. Volume = $80 \times 40 \times 30$
   = 96 000 cm^3 *(1 mark)*
5. $\frac{1}{2} \times 5.2 \times 4.1 = 10.66$ cm^2
   (2 marks available — 1 mark for the correct method, 1 mark for the correct answer.)
6.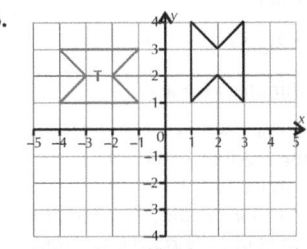
   (2 marks available — 1 mark for shape rotated 90° clockwise, 1 mark for correct position on grid.)
7. Area of metal
   = $\pi \times 3^2 = 28.2743...$ cm^2
   Area of hole = 12 cm^2
   Area of washer
   = $28.2743... - 12$
   = $16.2743... = 16.3$ cm^2 (3 s.f.)
   (2 marks available — 1 mark for a correct method, 1 mark for the correct answer.)

Geometry and Measures: Test 8

1. B *(1 mark)*
2. A *(1 mark)*
3.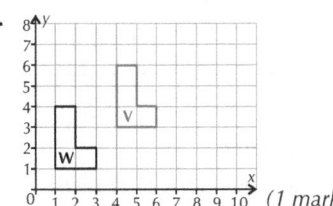
   (1 mark)
4. $180 \times (8 - 2) = 1080°$ *(1 mark)*
   $1080 \div 8 = 135°$ *(1 mark)*
5. Area of left trapezium
   = $\frac{1}{2}(8 + 4) \times 3 = 18$ m^2
   Area of right trapezium
   = $\frac{1}{2}(8 + 6) \times 5 = 35$ m^2
   18 m^2 + 35 m^2 = 53 m^2
   (2 marks available — 1 mark for finding the area of at least one trapezium, 1 mark for the correct answer.)
6. 50 cm = 0.5 m *(1 mark)*
   Area of circular face
   = $\pi \times 0.5^2 = 0.7853...$ m^2 *(1 mark)*
   Volume of cylinder
   = $0.7853... \times 7 = 5.4977...$
   = 5.50 m^3 (2 d.p.) *(1 mark)*

BONUS BRAINTEASER
$53 \times £15 = £795$

Probability and Statistics: Test 1

1. B *(1 mark)*
2. A *(1 mark)*
3. Negative correlation *(1 mark)*

Answers

4.
	1	2	3	4
1	2	3	4	5
2	3	4	5	6
3	4	5	6	7
4	5	6	7	8

(1 mark)

$\frac{3}{16}$ (1 mark)

5. Range = 96 − 65 = 31 (1 mark)
   Median: = 5th value = 82
   (1 mark)

6. $\frac{60}{360} = \frac{1}{6}$, so $\frac{1}{6}$ of the total number of students = 40
   So there are 40 × 6 = 240 students
   (1 mark)
   Jazz: $\frac{72}{360}$ × 240 = 48
   Ballroom: $\frac{144}{360}$ × 240 = 96
   Ballet: $\frac{84}{360}$ × 240 = 56
   (2 marks for all three values correct, otherwise 1 mark for one or two values correct.)

Probability and Statistics: Test 2

1. C (1 mark)
2. B (1 mark)
3. 8 (1 mark)

   July
   (1 mark)

4. 2 (1 mark)
   (0 × 5) + (1 × 5) + (2 × 8) + (3 × 7) + (4 × 4) + (5 × 1)
   = 0 + 5 + 16 + 21 + 16 + 5
   = 63 (1 mark)

5. $\frac{1}{6}$ (1 mark)
   $\frac{4}{6} = \frac{2}{3}$ (1 mark)

6. In order, the lengths are:
   1, 2, 3, 4, 7, 8, 12
   The median of all eight values lies between the 4th and the 5th values, so it will be before or after the 4. The median value is higher than 4, so it must be after the 4. 5 is halfway between 4 and the missing value, so the missing value must be 6.
   (2 marks available — 1 mark for a correct method, 1 mark for the correct answer.)

BONUS BRAINTEASER

Mean = total number of hats ÷ number of students = 63 ÷ 30 = 2.1

Probability and Statistics: Test 3

1. B (1 mark)
2. A (1 mark)
3. 75 minutes (1 mark)
4. 7 + 10 + 8 + 3 + 1 + 2 = 31,
   so the median = (31 + 1) ÷ 2
   = 16th value = 1
   (2 marks available — 1 mark for working out the position of the median, 1 mark for the correct answer.)

5. E.g.
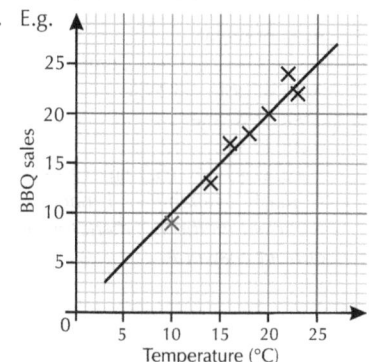
   (1 mark for all 6 points plotted correctly, 1 mark a correct line of best fit.)
   12 BBQs (allow 11-13) (1 mark)

6. Theme park or zoo
   = 90° + 45° = 135° (1 mark)
   $\frac{135}{360} = \frac{3}{8}$ (1 mark)

Probability and Statistics: Test 4

1. A (1 mark)
2. C (1 mark)
3. 20 − 7 = 13 counters are not red, so the probability of not red = $\frac{13}{20}$
   (1 mark)
4. Range = 84 − 4 = 80 (1 mark)
   Mode = 58 (1 mark)

5.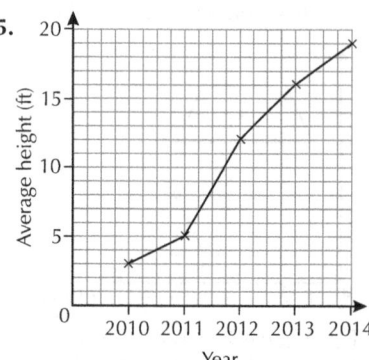
   (2 marks for fully correct frequency polygon, otherwise 1 mark for finding the mid-interval values.)

6. Number of holidays × frequency:
   0, 14, 20, 18, 16
   Total = 0 + 14 + 20 + 18 + 16 = 68
   Mean = 68 ÷ 40 = 1.7
   (3 marks available — 1 mark for completing the table, 1 mark for using a correct method and 1 mark for the correct answer.)